DEPARTMENT OF HEALTH AND SOCIAL SECURITY

KT-151-047

The Cherries Group Home:
A Beginning

D. G. RACE and D. M. RACE

LONDON: HER MAJESTY'S STATIONERY OFFICE

"From quiet homes and first beginning,
Out to the undiscovered ends
There's nothing worth the wear of winning
But laughter and the love of friends."

Dedicatory ode
Hilaire Belloc

The research project on which this book is based was financed
by the Department of Health and Social Security but the views
expressed are those of the authors and not necessarily of the
DHSS, or any other Government department.

ISBN 0 11 320343 8

Contents

Preface

This book stems from a research project into services for mentally handicapped adults, carried out in Berkshire during the period 1973–1977. The project, assisted by a grant from the Department of Health and Social Security, was divided into two distinct parts. The first part, known as the quantitative study, devised and used a measure of social competence to try and evaluate all the various living and working environments available to mentally handicapped adults in Berkshire. The second part, known as the qualitative study, examined in depth the development and functioning of an experimental group home called The Cherries. It is the second part which is the concern of this book.

While engaged on the research we were employed by the Operational Research (Health and Social Services) Unit at Reading University with one of us (D.G.R.) being jointly employed by that unit and Berkshire Social Services Department.

The fieldwork entailed very close cooperation and support from the Slough Division of Berkshire Social Services. In particular, the project required extensive use of diary material which involved the social workers concerned in a considerable amount of extra effort. We would therefore like to record our gratitude to the four social workers involved at various times in the project. The initial success of Liza Swift and Caroline Taylor was consolidated by Gerry Hufton and Rita Hill. Without them The Cherries project might never have got off the ground and this book would certainly not have been written.

Further thanks are due to The Cherries residents for putting up with us, and for allowing their experiences to be recorded for the benefit of others.

Lastly, we would like to thank Professor Robert Curnow and Mrs. Anne Parker for their comments and criticisms throughout the project, and in particular on the draft of this book. Needless to say, we take full responsibility for the views expressed hereafter.

D. G. Race
D. M. Race

Sheffield, *April 1978*

Introduction

Unlike the majority of the population, who usually have little interest in the subject, those involved with the mentally handicapped and with services for them have an almost pathological tendency for argument and dispute about what should be done to improve those services. Any new form of care, therefore, tends to be seized upon by everyone concerned with the problem, examined superficially, and then used as evidence to support totally opposing views.

It has been our aim in writing this book to try and create a more informed debate by providing greater detail of the development, problems and lessons to be learnt from one particular 'new' environment, The Cherries group home. Beyond this, however, we would also seek to inform a number of people who do not usually participate in the debate about services in general, but find the results of it applied to them. In particular, we are thinking of parents and relatives of mentally handicapped people. Through contacts with them in the course of our work we have found such people to be coping magnificently with their handicapped relatives, but often very much in the dark about possibilities for them.

We have also found a surprising lack of knowledge of the broader aspects of provision for the mentally handicapped by staff working in any one particular sector of these services. This, too, we hope to redress, since the book is intended for anyone at any level concerned in dealing with care for this particular group of people.

Though the book is primarily about one specific type of residential setting, it starts by providing a historical context into which The Cherries project can be placed. This leads on, in the second chapter, to the specific reasons for the building of The Cherries, and the aims and objectives surrounding the experiment. The bulk of the book is then taken up with a detailed narrative of the first three years of the group home, including, among other things, accounts of the lives of residents, the problems of living independently for the first time, the problems of being 'an experiment', and the benefits achieved during these three years. Considerable reference is made to a detailed diary kept by the social workers responsible for The Cherries as well as our own observations and experiences of the home.

We conclude the book with two chapters concerned with what we see as the results of The Cherries experiment, first looking at the achievements and problems of that particular home, and then expanding the argument to consider the lessons learnt from The Cherries about the place of group homes in the system of residential provision for mentally handicapped adults.

Throughout the book we have attempted to maintain confidentiality by the use of pseudonyms for individuals involved, but it is inevitable that anyone associated with The Cherries project will recognize some of the people described. We believe that no one will be offended by what we say, however, and we hope that, in any case, it will be realized how necessary a depth of personal information is in a proper examination of the issues arising from The Cherries.

CHAPTER I

Provision for the mentally handicapped – past and present

"Charity shall cover the multitude of sins" 1 Peter 4:8

Mentally handicapped people are typically marked out from the rest of their immediate society by an inability to cope satisfactorily in that society. Awareness of their problems, and the steps taken to remedy them, inevitably reflect the standards of behaviour demanded by society, and its tolerance of deviation from those standards. It is not surprising, therefore, that in underdeveloped countries the problem of mental handicap is little studied, still less provided for, since the level of poverty of the bulk of the population, combined with the less complex intellectual demands of a non-industrial state, means that the mentally handicapped are less susceptible to labelling as 'abnormal'.

As well as the lack of technological development, with its concomitant demands on the coping power of the individual, rural and tribal societies tend towards a greater acceptance of responsibility for the few severely handicapped of their members, and thus in the United Kingdom prior to the industrial revolution, the 'problem' of mental handicap did not exist as such. Most villages were able to cope with the 'idiots' in their midst, and sometimes at the expense of ridicule and exploitation, sometimes with an almost reverent regard for their simplicity.

With the industrial revolution, however, came large towns, the crowding together of workers dependent on the local factory, mill or pit for their livelihood, and the measuring of people by their ability to cope with new technological and commercial processes. In addition, there came an increase in education, and in the need for the more abstract skills of reading and writing if any sort of social status was to be achieved.

The mentally handicapped person thus began to stand out as being educationally and practically of low competence, but not, in the greater part of the nineteenth century, a specific threat to society, or a specifically undesirable person. Certainly, many handicapped people were incarcerated in workhouses, along with all the other unemployed or unemployable poor of most parishes, but there also prevailed a mood of optimism concerning the educability of those classified as idiots or imbeciles. Pioneering institutions of such as Guggenbuhl in Switzerland and Reed in England were designed as places where the handicapped could be kept in conditions amenable to their 'training and education'. The fact that the asylums also separated the handicapped from their

1

community was really secondary in the minds of the early workers. Their basic premise was that, given suitable attention and training, the idiot or imbecile was capable of learning simple tasks, sufficient to enable them to survive in certain parts of society. The prospects for development of this training and education therefore seemed bright, despite the fact that the confused terminology of the Lunatic Asylums Act of 1853 and the Idiots Act of 1886 meant that many authorities fulfilled their duties under the latter act to provide 'care, education and training' in special asylums by putting all their mentally disordered in the same place. However, the bright prospects of a developing service for the mentally handicapped were dimmed, at the turn of the century, by a complete change of outlook on the part of the leaders of opinion in the medical world. The change was, in essence, from optimism about the potential for education of the mentally handicapped to a belief that this education was not possible except in a very limited way and that the handicapped would always be a drain on society. To this pessimism was added the fear that the 'drain' would increase, because of supposed excessive reproduction amongst the handicapped. The idea of an inherited intellectual ability, which is unaltered by training or education, was not new at the turn of the century but it was in a minority view until the detailed work of Binet, attacking the 'empiricism' of his predecessors and calling for a 'scientific' approach to education, persuaded many of the invariance of basic 'intelligence'. Since he also provided them with a 'scientific' test with which to measure this inherent ability, it is not surprising that Binet's name is still associated with the 'innate intelligence' school and the opinions that certain people are 'ineducable' which held sway in this country for most of the first half of the century.

The opinion germinated by Binet at the turn of the century took hold of medical opinion and was fostered by the 'eugenic' ideas then beginning to circulate. Many studies appeared at this time which appeared to provide sound evidence of the inheritance of mental defect, together with the observation of a relatively high birth rate among the poor and handicapped sections of the population. This led to the view given by Tredgold, in his famous paper in the *Eugenics Review*[1] that segregation to prevent propagation was the only way to protect society. "I have come to the conclusion that, in the case of the majority of the feeble-minded, there is one measure, and one measure only, (to protect society) . . . namely the establishment of suitable farm and industrial colonies . . . Society would thus be saved a portion, at least, of the cost of their maintenance, and, more important, it would be secure from their depredation and danger of their propagation."

There is no doubt that this view was highly influential in the formation of the ensuing Mental Deficiency Act of 1913. At this time, all asylums were controlled by county councils, and their Boards of Control were

2

given powers under the new Act to prevent discharge of anyone they thought unfit to leave.

Section 2 of the Act provided the following conditions:

A person who was a defective might be dealt with by being sent to an institution for defectives or placed under guardianship.

"a. at the instance of his parent or guardian
b. if in addition to being a defective he was a person
   (i) who was found neglected, abandoned, or without visible means of support, or cruelly treated or . . . in need of care or training which could not be provided in his home; or
   (ii) who was found guilty of any criminal offence, or who was ordered to be sent to an approved school; or
   (iii) who was undergoing imprisonment, or was in an approved school; or
   (iv) who was an habitual drunkard; or
   (v) who had been found incapable of receiving education at school, or that by reason of a disability of mind might require supervision after leaving school."

If a parent or guardian was attempting to place their child in an institution they required two medical certificates from qualified medical practitioners, one of whom was approved for the purpose by the local health authority or the Minister of Health. The other reasons for a defective being sent to an institution i.e. b. above, could be cited by a number of people e.g. relatives, friends, or a local authority officer, in a petition to a 'judicial authority' again accompanied by two medical certificates. An order for admission lasted for one year. After that time the Board of Control was provided with reports on the defective person by the 'visitors' of the institution and by the medical officer of the institution, stating whether they should continue to be detained. If they were, the order was continued for a further year, and then for five year periods. The Board of Control retained the ultimate power to decide whether a defective should be discharged.

Although the caveat "in addition to being a defective" is used above, it is certain that, following the initial inertia brought about by the First World War, many people who had merely exhibited the behaviour described in section 2b, without necessarily being mentally handicapped, were committed to institutions. 'Certification' had a permanence about it, probably enhanced by the prevailing views of invariance of intellectual abilities and certainly compounded by the essentially subjective nature of the definitions of the Act. The motivation behind the Act was segregation of undesirable social 'inefficients' and, to a large extent, this was achieved. The Act applied to both children and adults, and part of the new power to be exercised by the Local Authority was to ascertain the numbers of children who were incapable by reason of

3

mental defect, of benefiting from the instruction in special schools or classes which had been set up in a small way under the Elementary Education (Defective and Epileptic Children) Act of 1899. Thus from an early age, the mentally handicapped could be certified as incapable of benefiting from any education, likely to be a burden on society, both in terms of draining its resources and lowering its stock, and thus subject to permanent detention in an institution. This is the extreme, of course, but it should also be remembered that the Mental Deficiency Act remained essentially the same until 1959, and thus there are many people, even nineteen years later, in institutions who were committed under this Act.

After the end of the First World War and for the ensuing twenty years, more and more people became 'subject to be dealt with' under the Mental Deficiency Acts. Tredgold[2] gives the following figures for those under the various forms of care provided by the Acts.

Table 1 **Total number of 'defectives' under the care and control of the Mental Deficiency Acts (source – Tredgold)**

Year	Total number (rounded)
1920	12,000
1926	37,000
1939	90,000
1950	100,000

The number requiring care between the wars rose more than seven fold and the pressure this put on the institutional services meant that, for primarily economic reasons, the size of institutions rose, until as O'Connor[3] notes "the tendency to build large institutions for about 2,000 patients in isolated country areas was a definite policy". He might have added that economy also brought about the conversion of large numbers of work-houses and lunatic asylums into the category of 'suitable' institutions. The essence of this policy, however, was, as Tredgold had demanded, for the large and isolated 'colony' to be set up. The *Wood Report*[4] published in 1929 sums up the position with frightening clarity. "The modern institution is generally a large one, preferably built on a colony plan, takes defectives of all grades of defect and all ages. All, of course, are properly classified according to their mental capacity and age. The Local Mental Deficiency Authority have to provide for all grades of defect, all types of case and all ages, and an institution that cannot, or will not, take this case for one reason and that case for another is of no use to the Authority. An institution which takes all types and ages is economical because the high-grade patients do the work and make everything necessary, not only for themselves, but also for the lower grade. In an institution taking only lower grades, the whole of the work has to be done by paid staff; in one taking only high grade the output of work is greater than is required for the institution itself and there is difficulty in disposing of it. In the all-grade institution, on the other hand, the high-grade patients are the skilled workmen of the colony, those who do all the higher processes of manufacture, those on whom there is a considerable measure of responsibility; the medium grade patients are the labourers, who do the more simple routine work in the training shops and about the institution; the rest of the lower-grade patients fetch and carry or do the very simple work."

The inter-war years were not, of course, noted for great developments in enlightened attitudes to the unfortunate members of society. Economic pressures brought a much more demanding dichotomy between the 'deserving' and 'undeserving' poor, and the hard times can be said to have had their effect on thinking in the mental handicap field. The combination of the prevailing view of permanent inadequacy with, it must be remembered, a service which depended on maintenance of numbers for continued financial support, left little changed by the end of the Second World War.

After the Second World War, however, research findings began to have some influence on opinion regarding the potential for employment of the mentally handicapped. It is interesting to note that most of these studies originated from outside those contemporary bodies with direct responsibility for the institutions in which most of the handicapped were housed, whereas within the direct caring profession the pessimistic pre-war views were maintained. This is important when consideration is given to the fact that those undergoing training in the forties and fifties are now in positions of considerable responsibility within the system of care provision for the mentally handicapped. Under the National Health Service Act of 1946 control of certified institutions passed from local councils to the Minister of Health and, through him, to the Regional Hospital Boards set up by that Act 'Colonies' became 'hospitals' overnight and trainee nurses, administrators, and doctors in the new health service would consider in their studies the accumulated wisdom of forty years of segregation. Tredgold seems to take most of the brickbats for the views of his day, but this is not surprising when statements such as those found as late as the eighth (1952) edition of his 'Textbook' are considered in terms of their effect on the development of attitudes in current senior staff dealing with the mentally handicapped. Thus, on euthanasia of "the 80,000 or more idiots or imbeciles in the country" he writes[5] "These are not only incapable of being employed to any economic advantage, but their care and support, whether in their own homes or in institutions, absorb a large amount of the time, energy, and money of the normal population which could be utilised to better purpose. Moreover, many of these defectives are utterly helpless, repulsive in appearance, and revolting in manners. Their existence is a

5

perpetual source of sorrow and unhappiness to their parents, and those who live at home have a most disturbing influence upon other children and family life. With the present shortage of institutional accommodation there are thousands of mothers who are literally worn out in caring for these persons at home. In my opinion it would be an economical and humane procedure were their existence to be painlessly terminated." Even on a less contentious matter than preservation of the 'fitter' stock, one of the issues on which the world had just gone to war, students in the forties and fifties would read on the matter of employability that "we may at once dismiss idiots and imbeciles, for, although the latter may be occupied in certain routine tasks, their financial value is practically nil".

In Education, too, the 1944 Education Act, set up with some considerable influence from Burt, had continued to define a class of children as "incapable of receiving education at school" and these were to be excluded from the 'universal' education system set up by that Act.

Thus within the professions of those involved with direct caring for the mentally handicapped, the pessimism of the inter-war years remained. From others, mainly psychologists in England, came findings which suggested that improvements were possible at all levels of defect. These, combined with direct observation and several inquiries into the state of mental hospitals in the fifties, led to a change of view in some quarters to something approaching optimism for patients' capabilities, and criticisms of the perceived inadequacies of the existing provision for them.

With the backing of their own studies, researchers were not only demonstrating the potential ability of the handicapped, but were beginning to criticise, either implicitly or explicitly, the facilities for care in existence during the fifties. One of the most famous studies of the 'Brooklands' Unit[6,7] confirmed the view of what might be called 'psychologists group' on the effectiveness of existing provision. This was, in summary, that hospitals were badly designed to meet the requirements of effective rehabilitation, and, in some cases, contributed to the deficiency of the individual.

The change of mood among research workers was, therefore, well established in the fifties, to one of confidence in the abilities of mentally handicapped people to respond to training and fulfil useful tasks in industrial employment. This did not, however, transmit itself to most of those directly involved with caring for the handicapped and it is significant that the major causes of the "Royal Commission on the Law Relating to Mental Illness and Mental Deficiency" and subsequent legislation were the more negative ones of bad conditions in hospitals and allegedly wrongful detention of certain people. The bad conditions were reported in terms of general inhumanity to the inmates, rather than a lack of opportunity for rehabilitation. The National Council for

Civil Liberties[8] published details of several cases of alleged wrongful detention under the 1913 Act which, together with the activities of the newly formed National Association for Parents of Backward Children (now the National Society for Mentally Handicapped Children) brought public attention to the way the Mental Deficiency Acts were operating and to the sort of institutions in which people were being detained. A report of the King Edwards Hospital Fund in 1955 summarised the position.[9] "In general it may be said that the average age of the mental hospitals is well over 50 years and that the majority date from the time when the mentally ill (sic) were looked on primarily as potential dangers to the community . . . some of these nineteenth and early twentieth century buildings and airing grounds suggest that 'prison' would be a truer designation even than 'asylum'. Second to the protection of the community came the custodial care of the inmates. These were herded in enormous wards, of a size not found in any other type of hospital, with cells for the solitary confinement of the more disturbed patients. Sometimes dormitories were provided for the patients from two or three wards and contained perhaps 160 beds or more in close-packed rows. Patients were not expected to have any possessions, and no lockers were provided. In some hospitals the patients' clothes are still rolled into bundles and tied to their beds at night, since no storage space is provided for them. Washing, bathing and toilet facilities were primitive and inadequate, even by the standards of the last century, and, in some cases, have remained so until the present day. Overcrowding occurs to a degree unknown in other hospitals".

The extremely poor physical conditions and the permanent detention of patients was, therefore, the main motivation behind the pressures for change given in the evidence to the Royal Commission. Though the report of the Commission spends some time on the idea of a move towards 'community care', the major conclusions, and the major effect of the 1959 Mental Health Act, was to abolish, except in certain defined circumstances, the compulsory detention of the newly, and confusingly, created categories of 'mentally disordered' persons. 'Informal admission' and the removal of 'certification' were the two key measures in what became known as the 'open door' policy, and much of the Act is taken up with procedures for compulsory admission, courts of protection and review tribunals etc. In terms of provision, no specific methods of care are proposed, the only clue to action being in paragraph 6 of the Act, wherein local health authorities are required to exercise an existing duty of section twenty-eight of the National Health Service Act 1946 for 'disordered persons' in the following way[10]:

"a. the provision, equipment and maintenance of residential accommodation and the care of persons for the time being resident in accommodation so provided.

7

b. the provision of centres or other facilities for training or occupation, and the equipment and maintenance of such centres.
c. the appointment of officers to act as mental welfare officers under
   the following provision of this Act.
d. the exercise by the local health authority of their functions under
   the following provisions of this Act in respect of persons placed
   under guardianship thereunder . . . and
e. the provision of any ancillary or supplementary services for, or for
   the benefit of any such persons as are referred to in subsection (1)
   of this Act."

It is worth noting that this provision is imposed as a duty on the public
health authorities, then part of the local government service. In practice
local interpretation of the duty to provide 'residential accommodation'
and 'training or occupation' was, in some cases, restricted merely to the
appointment of mental welfare officers to deal with admissions to, and
discharges from, the local mental hospital. Thus the care of those in
need of accommodation tended to remain in the hands of the hospital
service as administered by regional hospital boards. Hospitals,
incidentally, were now 'undesignated' i.e. they could admit all forms
of 'mentally disordered' persons, both the mentally ill and mentally
handicapped.

Other local authorities did make more of an attempt to meet their
prescribed duties under the Act, but were, of course, suffering from the
lack of a base of capital provision on which to build. Thus, with the
'residential' side taken care of by hospitals, those authorities doing
anything at all after the 1959 Act tended to concentrate on setting up
training centres, both 'Junior' for the 'ineducable' mentally handicapped children and 'Adult' for all mentally handicapped people over the
school leaving age (then 15).

For many reasons, therefore, the 1959 Mental Health Act was
unpopular to a significant group of those concerned with the mentally
handicapped, the major reason being that it effectively maintained the
status quo of the large hospital as the alternative in terms of residence to
keeping the handicapped person at home. The stigma of 'certification'
had been removed, some of the fears of 'unlawful' detention had been
removed, but the institutions remained. As in the fifties, the major
disagreements came from outside the direct caring services. From
within the profession, which mainly meant the psychiatric consultants,
sentiments were much more mixed. Some of this group were opposed to
any infringement of the right of the clinician to the ultimate decision
over the provision of service, and viewed with alarm the planned
number of 'hostels' being allowed into the ten-year plan for England
and Wales published in 1962. Hostels were, in any case, not yet in an
established form, and the only definition in operation by the end of the
fifties was essentially that of 'residential accommodation in small units'.

However, by comparison with hospitals of five hundred beds and more, quite a large number may be considered 'small'. Generally, however, hostel size became determined by a mixture of cost-conscious efforts at economics of scale, published material on the likely numbers requiring care in a local authority setting, and reproduction of an established pattern of size of provision for other long stay groups e.g. elderly people. A major influence on the future design of hostel provision was the experimental unit set up at Slough by the National Society for Mentally Handicapped Children[11]. Although the 'Slough experiment' had a much wider intention than mere residential care, being combined with an on-site training centre and run as an experiment in 'social training' for maximum functioning in the community, there is no doubt that the residential facilities at Slough had a considerable influence on the size of hostels over the next decade. This is not to give the impression of a spate of new buildings in the sixties. As mentioned earlier, many authorities, faced with the choice between training centres for the many or hostels for the few, chose to invest in the former, and by the time of publication of *Better Services for the Mentally Handicapped*[12] in 1971 the government admitted that "residential accommodation is still far short of what is needed". Thus, in the sixties, the bulk of the mentally handicapped in need of residential accommodation contained to be housed in hospital. To use one particular set of figures for the moment, from the 1971 White Paper[13], 52,100 in-patient beds were provided in 1969 for adults in NHS hospitals for the mentally handicapped, and 4,850 places in 'community' residential care. The latter figure includes various forms of accommodation, and is not totally made up of new buildings. Given this sort of difference in quantity of provision, it is not surprising that much influence on the development of services in the sixties continued to be exercised by the medical profession, maintaining the 'medical model' of care for the mentally handicapped as the service for the majority with a selected few subjects to the new provision of 'community care' in hostels and local authority training centres.

This was despite more studies being published on the success of rehabilitation experiments and the continuing debate on the appropriateness of an institutional environment to provide the sort of training necessary for such rehabilitation.

As well as specific studies, several authors joined the debate on a general level. As usual, there is a variation from very little hospital care being proposed to very little community care, and this seems to depend on the authors proximity to the hospital service. In fact, very few alternatives to hospital care existed, and the rehabilitation debate turned to the more detailed subject of the appropriate orientation of training rather than the general discussion of whether the right sort of basic residential provision was being planned.

In practical terms, therefore, though the experiments of the fifties had demonstrated the abilities of the mentally handicapped to learn social and industrial skills given adequate training and a stimulating environment, the sixties were noticeable more for debate on the desirability of rehabilitation, a joint approach to care, and the appropriate training to be carried out, than for any real changes in the pattern of direct care provision. This was especially true, as noted earlier, in the case of residential provision, where the large subnormality hospital continued to have a dominant influence on the type of care provided. It is therefore not surprising that studies continued to be published re-affirming the criticisms of existing institutions and pleading for more stimulating environments for the handicapped, and that the findings of Pauline Morris's large scale study of hospitals should have received such attention[14]. In this study, the author reported on a sociological survey of thirty-five subnormality hospitals in England and Wales which had as its objective "to discover what is actually happening in a given situation as well as what is said to be happening, or what is thought ought to be happening".

Her findings were highly critical of the provision for the mentally handicapped in subnormality hospitals and though she notes the state of transition of services for the handicapped in terms of 'concepts of care', her overriding conclusion, in agreement with the view expressed above, is that "if the philosophy of treatment is changing, our findings clearly indicate that this is not paralleled by similar changes in the provisions available for subnormal patients".

Although Morris's report cast grave doubt on the hospital, at least as then organized, as the appropriate environment for the mentally handicapped, it was again more basic failings of particular hospital regimes which drew public attention to the problems of the handicapped in hospital. In fact, Morris's book appeared shortly after one of a number of enquiries into psychiatric hospitals which were to appear over the ensuing years (this particular enquiry, into allegations of cruelty and neglect, was published as the How Report[15]) and for a short time the matter was given the full glare of national publicity. This had little effect in practice however, beyond optimistic statements of intent, and the debate returned to the level of published argument between the various groups associated with the handicapped. The spectrum ranged, as before, between those who argued for complete community care, except for a small number in need of direct nursing in general hospitals and those who sought to maintain the control and responsibility for the mentally handicapped in the hands of the medical consultant.

Events seemed, at the end of the sixties, to be moving towards the 'radical' solution, at least in theory. The report of the Seebohm Committee[16] and the subsequent legislation setting up Social Services Departments provided that 'social care' i.e. community care, should be the responsibility of these new bodies. The Seebohm Report also proposed the abolition of the idea of ineducability, and the takeover of the existing 'Junior Training Centres' by the education service. This was implemented in the Education (Handicapped Children) Act of 1970 which gave local education authorities the responsibility for educating all children, regardless of handicap.

Thus local authority services, except education, became the responsibility of the new Social Services Departments, and they were to take over those hostels and adult training centres in existence in the early seventies. However, as the Seebohm Report noted, "Published plans suggest that for years ahead many parts of the country will not have resources to provide adequate community care services" and the mere continuation of the existing level of provision did not satisfy the critics of the hospital-based system. The pressure of their arguments must have been felt in the senior levels of the Department of Health and Social Security since the White Paper *Better Services for the Mentally Handi-capped* published in 1971, gave much credit to the principle of rehabilitation in the community, and noted the 'deficiencies' of the current system.

Having done this however, and reviewed the arguments and findings considered above, its conclusions were considered by many to be half-hearted and lacking any real sense of motivation towards effective change[17,18]. Whilst advocating a reduction in hospital beds for adults from some ninety per cent of residential provision to just over forty per cent, the White Paper does not really explain why this remaining forty per cent are needed, and whilst advocating enormous expansion of local authority services, it gives no firm guidelines on the problems of transferring patients from hospitals to the community or on the appropriate type of accommodation for community provision. Beyond this, of course, it is an advisory document which has no force of legislation behind it, and thus individual local authorities and individual hospitals were left to follow its recommendations as freely as they wished.

Thus reactions from both sides of the fence were hostile. The 'radicals' criticised the White Paper for not going far enough and having no force behind it[19], while the psychiatrists group criticised the fact that their responsibilities were being diminished in response to 'unqualified' pressure[20]. The major criticism that we would make of the White Paper is its naive assumption that the sort of joint planning and organization necessary for its 'comprehensive' service would be possible with the continued existence of three entirely separate bodies, i.e. hospital boards, education departments and social services departments.

In practice there has been a steady growth in local authority services for the mentally handicapped, and a small diminution of the hospital population. Summary figures from a recent consultative document[21], show the number of residential care places in England in local authority private and voluntary homes rising from 5,900 in 1969 to 9,500 in 1974 and the hospital population falling from 60,000 in 1969 to 55,000 in 1974. Since the final targets of *Better Services* are 33,700 community places and 33,000 hospital places by 1991, considerably faster rates of growth and reduction will be necessary over the ensuing period. This is unlikely, given the current economic climate and the continuing debate over the responsibility for care and the appropriateness of particular types of care. There is a body of opinion[22,23,24], for a unified service to supersede the roles currently undertaken by the social, education and health services. Others[25] do not go as far as proposing a new service, but stress the importance of the 'multi-disciplinary team' approach to dealing with the mentally handicapped. The problem with this latter approach seems to be the divisions caused by the relative status of the team members[26]. Shapiro[27] maintains that the psychiatrist is the natural leader of such a team, a view not shared by opponents of the 'medical model' of care[28]. Given the relative status of clinicians and such people as social workers or residential care staff in the minds of the public at large it is scarcely surprising that hard attitudes are still adopted on both sides. The reality of provision, however, seems to be, as Tyne[29] points out, that despite a quarter of a century of research and debate on the appropriateness of existing care methods, there is no clear national policy for the mentally handicapped. "There have been changes. Yet the pattern of services available to a person with a mental handicap and his family is much the same as it always was. Hospitals are still large and distant from the people they serve. Local authorities have improved educational provision, but there is still pressure on day places in adult training centres. Residential provision has developed slowly and in a stereotyped way."

What, then, are the services available to a mentally handicapped person in 1978? It is noticeable, in several works on provision for mental handicap published in the late sixties and early seventies, that the author refers to an inability to describe current practice since the service is in a state of change. This is undoubtedly still true, and even if one restricts the changes experienced to the organizational ones of the setting up of Social Services Departments in 1971, Local Government Reorganization of 1974, and the National Health Service Reorganization of the same year, the effects on the groups of people receiving services from local and national authorities must be considerable. Therefore, a description of services currently available must be tempered with the caution expressed by other writers. However, since the purpose of this book is to examine the functioning of one sort of service for the adult mentally handicapped as a change from current provision and existing short-term plans, some description of what exists is necessary. As the emphasis of the book is towards mentally handicapped adults, however, no detailed description of services for children will be given here, with only the major provision being outlined.

Before school age, practically the whole contact of the parents of a mentally handicapped child with the professional caring services will be with the health services. This may come either through the maternity services immediately following birth, or through the health visitor and similar domiciliary services in the early years of the handicapped person. Often in the past, and still with some frequency, the handicap is not diagnosed at birth, and it may thus be the health visitor who actually carries out the initial diagnosis. Subsequent assessment by 'specialists' is still very variable as a recent working party of parents and professionals noted[30], and a wide variety of opinions concerning care may be given to the parents. In terms of actual resources before school age is reached, these normally amount to the choice between hospital or home care, with daytime activities occasionally being provided by playgroups organized from the voluntary sector. Since the Education (Handicapped Children) Act of 1970 all children of school age must be provided with educational facilities, regardless of handicap. This is normally undertaken in special schools which have extended from the old 'Educationally Subnormal' or 'ESN' schools, existing prior to 1970 for all but the most severely handicapped, to a two tier system of ESN(M) and ESN(S) schools, the latter being for the most severely handicapped, and taking over from the old Junior Training Centres. Some successful attempts have been made to place mentally handicapped children in normal schools, or in schools for children with other handicaps[31], but these remain a small minority. A few local authorities provide hostel places for children, some as a means of relief to parents on a short-term basis, others for more long-term care, and these hostels generally have between twelve and twenty-four beds. Other authorities restrict their community support to parents to visits from social workers. In general, beyond the provisions of education, services for children tend to vary in type and to come from different sources depending on the particular part of the country in which the parents happen to live.

Moving on to current services for adults, the picture is more confused. The statutory duty imposed on local education authorities to provide schools for mentally handicapped children has at least ensured some degree of equality of resources across the country for the day time care of school age children. After leaving school, not only does the provision of residential care come from different sources, but so too does the provision of training and employment.

Dealing with residential care first, the choices available to a mentally handicapped adult in most local authorities are his own home, a hospital or hostel. In his own home he theoretically receives the support of the local authority via their social workers. In a hospital he is under the care of the Regional Health Authority via the Area Health Authority

13

controlling the hospital, and in a hostel he is normally under the direct care of the local authority Social Services Department. Having said that these are the main choices may imply that the choice exists in all authorities. In fact, as the 1971 White Paper notes, progress in local authority residential care for the mentally handicapped up to that point had been very slow. Figures for the period between 1969 and 1974[32], show a rise of 3,600 adult places, from 4,200 to 7,800 in local authority and other community residential care, an increase from 9 places per 100,000 to 17 places per 100,000. This appears to be a rapid increase and it is true that the major impetus of the White Paper was to provide capital grants for the building of hostels for adults. Because of current economic stringency on Local Authority spending, however, this capital provision has now dropped, and a number of recently completed hostels are standing empty because of the lack of revenue finance to staff them[33]. However, as the two major sources of residential care outside the home available at present it is necessary to look in more detail at the type of provision meant by 'hospital' and 'hostel' care in 1978.

The local authority hostel, has, in the view of some, taken on something of its own institutional character. In the early days after 1971 the use of converted buildings led to a wide variety of sizes but, more recently, the 24–26 bedded purpose built establishment has become the stereotyped pattern of architectural design, largely, according to one architect[34] as a result of the guidance of DHSS architects and "because past models of care have been unquestionably copied. . . . It would seem that the possibility of providing ordinary housing had not been seriously considered on the whole". It is certain that the debate on 'stimulating environments for the handicapped' has resulted in some architects using the available resources to test out their own theories of environmental therapy without ever questioning the basic size of the unit prescribed. Other reasons which have been offered for the 24-bed hostel are the greater convenience of staffing arrangements, in that relief and shift work can be organized on a more economic staff/resident ratio than would be the case in a small group.

Whatever the reasons, it is the case that the vast majority of new local authority residential accommodation is in the form of purpose built 24–26 bedded units, with up to four resident staff, having a variety of titles including houseparents, officers-in-charge and wardens. Because of the hostels' size, they are not always part of conventional residential settings, except when built into new estates, and are often set apart in odd corners of land, these being the only sites available to local authorities. Thus the encouragement of the White Paper to local authorities to make their homes part of the community is made that much more difficult to achieve. These are only early findings and cannot be generalized too much, since hostels have been in existence for less than ten years in any numbers and have yet to settle down fully into an

14

established pattern of care, but the words of Professor Clarke have the ring of truth to them[35]: "authorities have more often been bewitched by the need for splendid new buildings rather than planning splendid new programmes which are the more important".

The pattern of care in hospitals, the major alternative to hostels as a residential care setting, is only too well established. The various studies over the years into hospital provision for the handicapped have already been described, and the real question at the moment is whether the hospitals of 1978 still fit the consistently critical picture found in these earlier works. Circumstantial evidence points to a pessimistic view. A number of public enquiries since 1970, have been highly critical of practices at certain subnormality hospitals[36,37] and detailed figures for 1973[38] show that out of the 71 hospitals for the mentally handicapped in England and Wales with over 200 beds, only four were above all departmental minimum standard levels for staffing, patients' amenities, and size of dormitories. Nineteen of these hospitals had either no personal cupboard space or no personal clothing for their patients and twenty had dormitories with more than 20 beds for children and 30 beds for adults. Staffing levels of one sort or another (medical, nursing or orderlies and domestics) were below the minimum level in 62 of the 71 hospitals, mainly in the orderly and domestic category. Only 5.8 per cent of all mental handicap hospitals in England and Wales had less than 100 beds, with one region, Newcastle, having no hospitals of less than 200 beds. Sixty-seven per cent of hospitals had over 500 beds.

In the same year 56 per cent of patients of all ages were engaged in some kind of occupational activity, though only about seven per cent of these activities were located outside the hospital setting. It is true that, following the White Paper of 1971, money was spent on improving the physical standards of subnormality hospitals, and the introduction of smaller units within hospitals and outside, known as 'Crossman's units' in some quarters, after the then Minister responsible, took place in some authorities.

However, seven years after the White Paper, many large institutions remain, with facilities below the departmental minimum standards of care, and the impression remains that the criticisms of earlier writers may still be valid. A slightly more recent survey of subnormality hospitals, using a checklist of 'desirable facilities'[39] concluded that "one thing is certain – no hospital would be able to answer yes to all the questions. . . . Overcrowding is a problem common to all. . . . Staff accommodation, in some hospitals, is totally inadequate as well. Supporting staff are thin on the ground, both on the domestic, teaching and other fronts and many institutions are struggling with archaic buildings and inadequate services." These views are reinforced by the survey of a hospital region by Professor Jones and her team[40], who, though claiming a new approach and not just looking at 'what was wrong' were forced to the same opinion as Morris's earlier survey over such matters as staff numbers, staff attitudes, total resources, and general integration with the community. Thus, ten years later than the 'Put Away' survey, Jones and her team reveal the same inadequacies in the hospital service displayed by Morris. They conclude[41] "The 1971 White Paper was intended to open the door: to produce a new situation . . . but if the door has been opened, it is only by a crack. . . . There have been some gains – the small 'Crossman units' and the injection of money into furnishings and ward decoration; a spirit of determination and goodwill among some nurses, which has improved the living conditions of many 'high-grade' patients. These advances, however, have been offset by a declining morale among many hospital staff, born of the belief that nursing the mentally handicapped is 'not really nursing'; that the traditional leadership has gone and left a vacuum; and that, in the event of a public inquiry, it is the ward staff who will be left to carry the blame for situations largely beyond their control."

On the other side of the spectrum of opinion, several studies of patients currently in subnormality hospitals made by psychiatrists put forward the view that the in-patient population is getting worse and that demands for hospital care are increasing. It is their opinion that the majority of the 50,000 patients in hospitals "have no prospect of being able to live in the community", and thus that "hospitals must remain responsible for this group for the foreseeable future". It is not possible, they claim, to run down admissions to the hospitals because the numbers of the severely subnormal surviving to middle age is increasing, and by age 45 almost all require hospital care. Therefore the "hospital requirements will be significantly greater". They further conclude that "Certain hospitals represent centres of excellence in the care of the mentally handicapped in the provision they make in medical, para-medical and nursing spheres."[42] Since these are the views of those who, in their own words "reject, in the context of the hospital services, the suggestion . . . that mental handicap should be regarded as a social or educational responsibility rather than a health one" and maintain that "there are no areas in the management of patients in hospital that do not come ultimately under his (the consultant's) aegis" it seems likely that the conditions of patients in hospital under this 'management' will remain at a similar level to those sanctioned by the 'management' of ten years ago. It is important to recognize the power behind the consultants' views when estimating the likely changes in hospital services since the last directly observed studies. Indeed, they themselves admit that there are "iniquitous living and working conditions still existing in many hospitals throughout the country" and the inevitable conclusion must remain the same as that expressed earlier; very little change has occurred in the treatment of those in hospital when considered against the general progress of knowledge in the mental handicap field, and the detailed pictures of hospital environments drawn by Morris, Jones, Goffmann and others remain essentially accurate today.

As stated earlier, hostels and hospitals constitute the great majority of residential provision for the mentally handicapped outside their parental home. Other than these two types of care, a few experiments have been attempted in residential services, although none have been firmly established nationally. The two main types of residential care under this heading have been group homes, a name normally applied to establishments where a small group of mentally handicapped people live without residential supervision, and lodgings, where ex-patients or others are placed in commercially run boarding houses. The former will be dealt with in detail in the rest of this book, while the latter, lodgings, have proved a more controversial alternative to hostel care in a number of local authorities. Professor Jones[43] found them to be "often used as a dumping ground for those for whom hostel places were not available or, who did not fit into the fairly middle-class ethos of hostel life" and concluded that "Except in certain outstanding cases, accommodation in lodgings was very often unimpressive and sometimes of a very poor quality". A number of scandals about 'decanting' from mental hospitals have, more recently, been the subject of national press coverage, often with a great deal of confusion between mental illness and mental handicap, and certain cases of abuse have been discovered. Even more than in most types of residential care, the pattern of life in lodgings is determined by the individual landlord, and thus the uncaring profiteers are to be contrasted with genuinely concerned individuals. The problem seems to be a lack of control by the caring services over people in lodgings, without an adequate means of ensuring that the handicapped people have sufficient self-control to be able to benefit from the increased independence. Some successes have been achieved however[44].

As a whole then, residential services for mentally handicapped adults consist and certainly consisted in the early seventies when The Cherries was being designed, of a straight choice between hostels and hospitals. As the next chapter will show, The Cherries was to evolve into a type of residential care very little considered; a home of one's own.

CHAPTER II

The development of The Cherries

"The distance doesn't matter, it is only the first step that is difficult" Marquise du Deffand

In the late 1960's Slough Society for Mentally Handicapped Children (Slough Mencap) were concerned about the lack of provision for a group of mentally handicapped people known to them. This group were aged from about 25 to 40 and most were holding down jobs in the community, although a few were attending adult training centres. The worries of the society arose because this group of people were all living with fairly elderly parents who felt that they would not be able to cope with their offspring for much longer.

Neither the parents nor the society felt that these people required the amount of supervision that was provided by a hostel or hospital, and they also wished to provide something more homely than either of these for their sons and daughters. While the parents were obviously most concerned about the future for their children, Slough society were aware of other aspects of the debate about community care mentioned earlier, and in a discussion document produced in 1970 the following points were raised in support of their idea to build a group home.

1. It would provide accommodation that would be self-financing or very slightly subsidized for people who would otherwise cost the state a large amount to house in hostels or hospitals.
2. Residents would be living near their previous homes and so be able to continue working in the community contributing to the national wealth.
3. The group home could provide accommodation for married mentally handicapped people without children for whom no accommodation was currently provided.
4. It would help solve part of the problem caused by the shortage of house-parents or wardens for hostels.
5. It would provide conditions that would foster the attainment of a higher degree of independence among adult mentally handicapped people than was then possible.
6. It would provide a more satisfying life for the people thus accommodated.

Mencap referred to experiences in Sweden as a reference for their final two points, and presumably had in mind the idea of 'normalization' expressed by such people as Grunewald[45]. "Normalization does not

imply any denial of the retarded person's handicap. It involves rather exploiting his other mental and physical capacities, so that his handicap becomes less pronounced. It means also that the retarded person has the same rights and obligations as other people, so far as this is possible."
Applying this principle to residential accommodation would mean that wherever possible mentally handicapped people should have the opportunity to grow up and leave home, but leave home to live in a small group, rather than a large institution.

At the same time as the discussion document was produced Slough society set up a working party to plan the details of the home. This group eventually decided that the home should have places for ten residents plus some accommodation for a 'next-door-neighbour' which was to be convertible to accommodation for further mentally handicapped people (possibly a married couple) in the future. The idea behind the proposal for a 'next-door-neighbour' was that when the residents moved in to the home they would initially require some help in adjusting to the demands of life without direct parental support. As they became more self-sufficient the 'neighbour' would be able to ease himself out of the situation thus leaving the accommodation free for further mentally handicapped adults.

With their ideas formulated Slough Mencap approached an architect, Mr Kenneth Bayes, and he agreed to draw up plans for the home. When these were approved the estimated cost of the house was £25,000, excluding the cost of the site. Before the society set about raising the money they approached Buckinghamshire County Council and offered them the home if the council would provide the site and the furnishings. Apart from the need to obtain a site for the house, Slough society felt that the home could be run more effectively and with more continuity of service by the local authority than by them. It would also open the home to those who were not members of the society, but who still could benefit from the type of provision being offered. The authority agreed to provide the site and so fund-raising could begin.

The fund-raising went ahead fairly steadily, with much of the money coming from public subscription and from various trust funds. Money was also provided by the DHSS on condition that research should be undertaken to evaluate the group home. Because of the generality of the expressed aims of the home, there were some difficulties in the initial design of the research programme and discussions went on for some considerable time to try and establish formal admission criteria and objectives for the home.

During this time there were also problems arising over the idea of the 'next-door-neighbour'. Mencap wanted the neighbour to be in the home only during the time that most working people are in their own homes, i.e. evenings and weekends. They did not feel it was necessary to provide constant supervision but only to limit the likelihood of major crises arising. However, Buckinghamshire Social Services Department felt that it was an almost impossible task to impose on anybody since the job demanded the ability gradually to ease out of a situation in which residents had learned to depend on the neighbour. They felt that it would be easier to provide visiting support with the visits being gradually reduced as the residents gained in competence, whereas a resident 'neighbour' would always be available, even though he were trying to encourage independence. There were also administrative difficulties involved in providing such a neighbour with fixed hours of duty, holiday entitlement, etc. The idea of there being no resident supervision worried Slough Mencap considerably and they felt the residents would need to be of such high social competence that they might just as well be in digs on their own.

The debate about the 'neighbour' continued for some time, and was finally resolved in August 1972. By this time the cost of the building had escalated to £50,000 and, if the home was to be built at all, something had to be omitted from the plans. It was agreed, rather reluctantly, and after promises of training programmes for the residents, that the accommodation for the neighbour was the least important part of the home and so this was cut. A site had been provided on the edge of a newly planned council estate so that the residents could not be faced with the problems of fitting into an established community. Thus in November 1972 The Cherries was able to be started.

Building went ahead, and, with very few delays, the house was completed by early August 1973. The house that was ready to be handed over to Buckinghamshire County Council had accommodation for twelve residents in two single and five double bed-sitters. Apart from storage and washing facilities the only other rooms were a small television lounge and a large kitchen/dining room. With two of the double bed-sitters on the ground floor, the whole house was designed to enable some physically handicapped residents to be accommodated. It therefore had wide doors and modern easy to use facilities in low positions for comfortable use from a wheelchair. The home also had a reasonably large garden.

While the building was in progress there were many meetings of The Cherries committee, containing representatives from the Buckinghamshire County Social Services Department, including their research team, and Slough Mencap to discuss the aims of the group home and try and establish admission criteria. The aims were formalized at a meeting in January 1973[46] as being to discover

1. Whether mentally handicapped adults can live without supervision
2. How low an I.Q. a person can have and still live in this way, and the admission criteria as:

General
Potential residents must:
1. be ready to try living in The Cherries
2. have local contacts and preferably have a home address in the area to be transferred to new Berkshire. (This because, with government reorganization most of the Slough area was to be transferred from Buckinghamshire to Berkshire)
3. be able to 'mix' in a group (this to be assessed during a trial period at Elliman House, the Slough local authority hostel)
4. have some occupation that takes him/her out during working hours
5. be continent, ambulant and have no severe behaviour disorders.

Domestic
Each resident must have the ability:
1. to dress, keep clean, toilet, wash, bath
2. to make their bed and clean and tidy rooms
3. to use money (i.e. small change and putting aside rent)
4. to handle their own medication.

It was, however, agreed that everyone did not need to be able to do everything, i.e. "the group as a whole will have pooled skills, so that the whole will be greater than the sum of the parts."

The Cherries committee also formalized the admissions policy that was to be adopted. A second committee containing representatives from Buckinghamshire Social Services Department, the research team, and Elliman House staff, but not parents, was to decide on admissions according to the following policy decisions

1. There should be a balance of the sexes in the home
2. There should be a balance of I.Q.'s above and below 50
3. There should be a period of pre-training at Elliman House (probably for a minimum of three months).

Although this new committee had been formed, future decisions about admissions policy and group home objectives were still to be decided by The Cherries committeee, since representatives of parents were still be be involved with the general running of the home.

By the time the group home was ready for the first residents, the criteria for admission had been extended and clarified, so that there was more detail about which were individual and which were group skills. The following list of criteria is the one used to select the first group of residents[47]:

Criteria for Admission
(A) Each individual must:
1. be continent
2. be ambulant

3. not have unacceptable behaviour, personality problems or mental illness
4. have a medical condition which is stable
5. be 18 years old or more
6. be in full-time employment or going to one of the adult training centres
7. be able to administer his or her own medication without supervision
8. be able to wash, dress and feed unaided
9. be able to make individual purchases from shops*
10. be able to retain appropriate element of income to pay rent*
11. be able to do basic household jobs
12. be able to get up and dress given reasonable prompting
13. be able to make a simple journey by bus
14. live within the Slough Mencap area and within the boundary of New Berkshire
15. want and need accommodation with less support than a hostel but more than in independent accommodation.

(B) At any time the group must have the following characteristics:
1. to be able to summon help by telephone
2. to be able to pay bills, especially rent and house-keeping
3. to be able to prepare meals with a reasonably balanced diet, and to clean up afterwards
4. to get up and off to work in time
5. an I.Q. balance to be maintained as follows:
Four places in the group home should be set aside for persons with an I.Q. of below 50. These may be filled at any time by persons with an I.Q. of below 50. There is no upper limit to the number of persons with an I.Q. below 50 who may be admitted. In the event that there are four vacancies or less at the group home and these are all set aside as described and there is a potential resident with an I.Q. of more than 50 who could otherwise take up this place, the vacancy should be kept for six months from the time of application for the person with an I.Q. of over 50. If no suitable resident with a lower I.Q. has been found by this time, the vacancy may be allocated. This will be taken to mean that the demand for this type of home is not yet established for the four places and only three will be set aside. This process may repeat.

It was felt that all potential residents would require some form of training before they could cope with independent living. Since the move to the group home would involve living together as a group, it seemed obvious that potential residents should receive this training while living

* A general idea is needed of what is required in these operations, but a complete, successful and unaided undertaking by the person, is not required.

22

in a group situation. The easiest method of achieving this was to move the people concerned into one wing of Elliman House hostel in Slough, where they could be given help in practical matters, while learning to adjust to one another.

The Cherries committee also realized that it was impractical to attempt to move twelve people into the group home at one time. They therefore decided that a batch system, whereby two or three small groups were processed consecutively through the hostel, was the answer. This would, it was hoped, fill the home, and then further vacancies, occurring as people moved on to ordinary accommodation, could be filled as they occurred. It was thought that these individuals, who were to move in later, need not necessarily pass through the hostel, but could receive whatever training they required, while staying in their own environment.

The admissions policy has changed since the opening of the home, but further discussion of this will be considered in later chapters, and not here, since it is intricately involved with the development of the group, and the way they reacted to the problems of moving to a new environment. There was, however, some documented statement of aims and admission criteria in existence at this stage but formal detailed objectives did not appear until a progress report, written for the transfer of responsibility from Buckinghamshire to Berkshire, was produced. In this report the objectives were summarized as follows[48]:

1. *Group Home as Home*
The main objective is to provide a place of residence for twelve mentally handicapped persons. The intention is that the residents should regard it as home, and no pressure should be put on them to move on to independent accommodation, although if they express a wish to do so, help in this should be given. The group home is not intended for persons already able to live in a less protected situation or in independent accommodation.

2. *Origin and Characteristics of Residents*
   a. the selection of residents is to be initially and principally from the Slough MENCAP area and within 'New Berkshire', but rather than keep places vacant, the search for residents may be extended into the rest of Berkshire.
   b. residents are to be of either sex
   c. residents should be at work either in open employment or at one of the Adult Training Centres
   d. the age of residents is to be generally young rather than old, but a diversity of ages within the group is desirable
   e. there is to be a wide distribution of I.Q. within the group, but with efforts made to encourage those with I.Q.'s below 50 to become residents.

23

3. *Support Services*

The group home is to be independent of residential support, but if necessary, to be given domiciliary help by social workers and home helps.*

4. *Finance*

The overall cost per resident was assumed to be lower than in alternative staffed accommodation, and an objective is to see how far this assumption was justified. The residents are to pay to the County Council an economic rent, supported, if necessary, by a Supplementary Allowance.

It is obvious that despite these stated objectives there were constraints upon the local authority which had to be taken into account, and which limited the scope for achieving the objectives. The major constraints were on the first objective and are described concisely in the hand-over report.[49]

"*Group Home as Home*. This is possibly the most important objective for the residents, but the most difficult to define and maintain. Successful attainment of this objective depends on the resolution of an essentially contradictory situation. On the one hand the residents are expected to have maximum independence and autonomy over their decision, life style and so forth. On the other, the local authority has a responsibility for the well being of the residents and cannot, in good faith, hand over all decisions to the residents. It is unlikely that any authority would actually do this, but it is extremely easy to say the residents have full independence, not recognizing the very severe limitations to that independence. For example, our department would not allow the group home to remain under-occupied, (against professional judgement), because the existing residents felt they did not want further members. Similarly, we did impose limits on the type of person that the residents might wish to have as new members. To act in any other way would be to disregard professional responsibility. Thus, even in a group home, there are considerable restraints on the extent it can be regarded as 'home'. This puts an additional responsibility on the local authority to recognize the areas in which it does have control of the use of the group home, and to exercise the control in a way that is as consistent as possible with 'home life'. In some areas, particularly in respect of day to day organization and household management, the residents will have much more autonomy. These areas, however, are hard to define, for in every case there are limits to the freedom of action which the local authority will allow and these limits may be broader or narrower than those normally adopted by the wider community."

* The support agreed upon finally was that one social worker should have particular responsibility for the home, to the extent of half her time. In addition each resident would have 'his/her own' social worker. It was also agreed that domicilliary help with housework should be non-existent or minimal to start with and increased as necessary.

24

Just how real the fears regarding the problems of a 'home' emerging from The Cherries were, will be examined as the book progresses, but this description of the beginnings of The Cherries will be concluded by a brief outline of the arrival of the authors into the scheme of things.

With the production of the hand-over report, the research team at Buckinghamshire Social Services Department also handed over formal responsibility for the evaluation of the home to the authors. Prior to this exchange a research proposal to the Department of Health and Social Security, of which a qualitative study of the development of The Cherries was a part, had been accepted. The research design concerning The Cherries was, quite simply, observation and monitoring of the progress of the residents and staff attached to the home by a variety of techniques but mainly by the use of extended diaries kept by the social workers involved with the project. In the chapters which follow, considerable use will be made of these diaries, as the story of The Cherries group home evolves.

CHAPTER III

Initial selection of residents

"I've got a little list" W. S. Gilbert – *The Mikado*

Faced with the prospect of selecting potential residents for The Cherries from the mentally handicapped in Slough, Buckinghamshire Social Services Department collected and reviewed information on a large number of individuals proposed by Slough Mencap. Established criteria for selection did not of course exist since, as can be seen from the first chapter, The Cherries represented a new concept in residential care. In these circumstances Buckinghamshire, quite understandably, used the only experience available to them, which came from the selection of residents for their hostels. Such selection tended to be on the basis of the potential residents' capabilities in the practical skills necessary for social acceptance, e.g. washing, dressing, lack of behaviour problems, etc. The criteria for The Cherries outlined in Chapter II was thus an extension of this practical assessment, with greater skills being demanded of potential Cherries residents. In addition, it was decided to restrict to six the first group to be admitted, in an attempt to keep the initial problems within manageable bounds.

Perceived failings in practical skills and a lack of the desire to move eliminated all but 18 of the initial group of about 90 reviewed by Buckinghamshire. These 18 were then studied in greater detail, and 12 were rejected as unsuitable for various reasons such as being 'too capable' or having difficult personalities. Two of the remaining group of six were rejected almost immediately because of personality problems which placed very severe demands on the group, and replaced by two others whose cases were reconsidered. This apparent arbitrariness is easily criticized with the benefit of hindsight, but condemnation should be restrained when it is remembered that not ten years had passed since the first hostels were opened, and that experience in selection for community living was extremely limited. Clearly the selection of residents at this stage was largely an act of faith and a fairly cautious policy was certainly the most likely to achieve success. Six candidates had emerged, however, and for their pre-admission training they were moved into a wing of the hostel in Slough. In this wing the six were provided with their own sitting room and kitchen, as well as the usual bedrooms and bathroom. Other members of the hostel were not permitted to enter these rooms except when invited to do so by a member of the group. Although four of the six had been residents of the hostel prior to this separation, surprisingly little animosity was aroused by the status of the group in training. Only one hostel resident, who had spent many years in hospital, disliked these alterations to the routine, exhibiting his disapproval by temper tantrums and in a vain attempt to set up a rival group.

Given the hopes and desires of Slough Society to provide accommodation for mentally handicapped people living with elderly parents in the community, it might seem somewhat surprising that four of the initial group of six were drawn from those currently living in the hostel. However, when The Cherries opened, parents were very reluctant to allow their offspring to be 'experimented on' in a new environment, and it soon became apparent that they wished to see the home working before they considered it as a possibility for their son or daughter. Thus the residents of the hostel became the most obvious candidates for The Cherries.

The purpose of separating the six potential residents at this stage was to try and prepare them as a group for admission to The Cherries when it opened, since it was felt that a cohesive group would have a better chance of moving in successfully than a collection of individuals. The practical emphasis of the selection procedure was continued into the training programme they were to follow, which had no formal structure but can be loosely described as follows:

Cooking: raw materials were provided to enable the group to become used to catering for themselves.

Cleaning: the group were responsible for looking after their wing of the hostel.

Laundry: use was made of the hostel facilities to encourage the group members to do their own washing and ironing.

Money: some instruction was given in the use of money for housekeeping, etc. However, it was difficult to give the group experience of budgeting in the sheltered environment of a hostel, since the cash available to residents is limited by the supplementary benefits rule which demands that most of the allowance be paid directly to the hostel. Thus experimentation in cash purchases, especially of food, could not be undertaken without some form of grant, which was not available.

Group meetings: these were organized on a regular, semi-formal basis, with at least one member of the hostel staff and the social worker attached to the group home present, in an attempt to encourage the group to take a responsible role in solving their own problems.

The items listed above are specific aspects of the training, but the sheer fact of living as a more self-sufficient group and being treated as such was assumed to have a beneficial effect on the residents' ability to cope with independent living.

27

The general household tasks were usually shared out amongst the members, although the work involved meant that there was little free time available to the group. The wing was kept 'immaculately' and, despite the fact that one member tended to do most of the cooking, the others assisted in preparation and occasionally gave her a day off. Meals were initially group affairs but by the end of a month, except for Sunday lunch and special occasions, individual catering was the rule. In fact, whilst in the first month the group coped adequately with the practical aspects of the training scheme, certain personality problems were beginning to emerge.

These were largely concerned with the problems experienced by potential residents of conceptualizing life in the group home itself, and anxiety over their ability to cope with an unknown situation. Indeed, while staff concerned were beset with questions about such worries as getting to work or keeping pets, it proved extremely difficult to get the group to work towards their own solutions. In other words they were still very much dependent on having ideas suggested to them, being unused to the necessity of solving their own problems. At this stage the potential residents had not yet seen the group home, which was in the final stages of being fitted out, and the feeling that the move to the group home was a step into the unknown was therefore increased. Such fears will always be a problem at the introduction of a completely new environment, and although it could perhaps have been slightly alleviated by a visit to the physical premises of The Cherries, the fundamental difficulty remains. There is, particularly with the mentally handicapped, a need for a 'working example' to allay many fears. Further evidence of this fact will be seen later.

As well as sharing in these general anxieties (she was the person worried about pets), Jenny* was presenting additional problems to the group. At this point a brief history of Jenny's background will be given. It will be policy throughout the book to introduce individuals with such histories in order to provide some insight into the parts they play in succeeding events.

*

JENNY

Year of birth 1950   I.Q. range 51–55†
Parents – father: engineer, mother: teacher

Few problems before 1966 when schooling (E.S.N.) finished. For five years at two hostels for most of the time, with occasional periods at home. Problems of crying, temper tantrums, pulling out hair whenever returning to the hostels, brought on by feelings of rejection. Since then has been at home permanently.

* All names in this book are fictitious.
† Further details of the dates and types of I.Q. test will be provided in Chapter IX.

Jenny had joined the group two weeks after the others and became increasingly demanding and attention-seeking over the ensuing weeks. "I felt that her behaviour might be her need to establish herself in this semi-established group" was the opinion of the social worker at the time, and this insecurity is borne out by her background. "Jenny would retire into whining and whimpering, constantly looking to see what effect she was having on the rest of the group". Behaviour of this type eventually caused her to be withdrawn from the group.

At the same time another of the residents, who was being given the opportunity to return home, decided that he would rather do this than face the problems of group home living. Thus the group was now reduced to four, Cathy, Susan, Martin and Derek. Other potential residents were still being considered, of course, though none were yet thought to be ready to join the pre-admission group. Social training continued, as evidenced by the following diary extract.

Cathy asked whether there would be a first aid kit down there, and this led to a long discussion on coping with emergencies. We assured Cathy that we would put a first aid kit in the home if one were not provided, and Cathy commented that it would be very difficult if there were no first aid kit there, because if someone were to burn themselves, that person would have to wait at the group home while somebody ran to the Chemist to ask them to sell them a bandage. I could hardly keep my face straight at this vision, and promised to look into this. This led on, naturally, to a discussion of fire and illness. We talked about what circumstances would necessitate the calling of an ambulance, and explained that they would be registered with a Doctor locally. Cathy brought up the subject of running a temperature and we talked about when one should stay in bed and call the Doctor and when one should go to the Surgery. Derek said that he knew how to take someone's temperature, and Cathy fetched her thermometer. Derek shook it down but Cathy was unable to see the line of mercury and, in the end, the hostel warden suggested that he could ask his wife to show them how to take a temperature when she was free.

Practical and emotional development, however, continued at different rates. Only finance proved a major practical problem, largely for the reasons given earlier, but on the behavioural side, the signs of an increase in anxiety were evident, together with indications of interpersonal problems within the group. The first person to suffer was Martin.

*

MARTIN

Year of birth 1949   I.Q. range 41–45

Parents – father: business man, stepmother: housewife

Lived at hostel for six years prior to being considered for the group home. During the last nine months of this period was in open employment. Father rarely at home due to business. Home is in rural area away from Martin's social contacts therefore not felt desirable that Martin should return.

Martin has been very friendly with the person who had returned home and appeared to miss his company. In fact he admitted as much in a group meeting. However, he seemed to be getting over this up to the time when the group were due to visit The Cherries for the first time. As he was perhaps the least capable member of the group he began to feel the pressures of coping alone were mounting and a severe bout of asthma was brought on. Subsequently, although he visited The Cherries, he no longer wished to go to the group home. This was a culmination of all the worries he had had regarding the venture, which he now, as a result of his friend's departure, had to bear alone.

The untried nature of The Cherries has been mentioned before, and difficulties were therefore experienced by staff, particularly those working in the hostel, in defining their attitudes to it. This resulted in a variety of attitudes being formed. Some of these did not lend themselves to a forceful approach to people such as Martin, and may even have led to discouragement. However, there is no evidence that a move for Martin at this stage would have been successful as the anxieties were most certainly present.

A similar problem presented itself in the case of Susan.

*

SUSAN

Year of birth 1950   I.Q. range 46–50

Parents: Divorced – father: overseas, mother: office worker

From living with parents and attending E.S.N. school Susan had moved to hostel six years before. Had become more independent and was reported as having "A pleasant personality and friendly disposition". Had been close friends with Cathy and Martin before group home venture and therefore wished to accompany them. Mother worried about not being able to cope with Susan and this anxiety is transmitted to Susan, who is a highly strung, nervous person.

Susan is small in stature and as such tends to be dwarfed by others as well as her surroundings. She has been worrying continuously about her mother's reaction to her admission to The Cherries, despite knowing that her mother had been informed that she was coping very well. Again staff attitudes were not always persuasive and the matter was made worse by the fact that Derek was tending to dominate, or even bully, her. "Susan confided that she was having problems with Derek who was extremely bossy, ordered her around and made her life a misery." At the first group home visit, the size of an empty twelve bedded house, set apart as it then was, proved the final straw, and after this visit she announced that she no longer wished to be a member of the group. Being Susan she then became very anxious about this and persuaded herself that people were trying to force her into the home. The social worker notes the interesting theory that she might in reality have been asking for someone to push her into the group home, i.e. to make the decision for her.

This left Cathy and Derek, who were still coping very well with the practical problems, though Derek's behaviour was giving cause for concern.

*

DEREK

Year of birth 1930   I.Q. range 41–45

Parents: both dead

Entered hospital 1942. Returned to live with mother 1962 and for ten years employed by Slough Corporation until his mother's death in 1972. Unable to cope on his own and was readmitted to hospital one month later. Employed at the hospital as a domestic help until moved to hostel early in 1973, when he obtained a job in the community. During period coping alone was given to uncleanliness and wandering.

From the early days of the group home group, Derek had shown signs of a slightly overbearing attitude to the others, particularly towards Susan.

"Derek remained very quiet during the meeting and did not appear to be paying a great deal of attention to what was being said. His only participation was when discussing an argument he and Martin had had about how the washing up should be done. He then came forward and defended his side of the argument and seemed quite unable to see that other people could have their ideas about how to do a job and might prefer to do things in their own way. He demonstrated a very rigid outlook and did not appear to be part of the group at all. It was noticeable that he sat between two members of staff."

Once again difficulties of independent decision-making and action by the group were highlighted. It transpired shortly afterwards that "Derek seems to be having a reign of terror but nobody had the strength to bring this up at the group meeting." How forceful this "reign of terror" was and how much it contributed to the decisions of Martin and Susan is difficult to assess. It is clear that Derek's attitude of conceit in his abilities did not make his training very easy. However, he survived Susan and Martin as a member of the group home group, and for a short period seemed to be adopting a more responsible attitude. Indeed, some talk of marriage with Cathy arose.

This not unnaturally brought up the matter of sex education, which was considered to be part of the overall social training. Both Derek and Cathy, despite some ignorance of the facts of life, displayed a responsible attitude towards sex in general. "Cathy then announced that she thought kissing and cuddling were all right, but that one should not go

31

any further, and I felt she was firm enough in her belief to avoid any disasters." The romance however was short lived and was already over by the time a decision had to be made on whether Derek should be admitted, in view of his bullying behaviour.

It was decided, after intense discussion, that of the two remaining group members "Cathy was fine for the group home but Derek was highly unsuitable." It had been made clear to all group members that the training period was also a period of assessment, and therefore there was no obligation to move Derek into the group home, but there were fears about his reaction to the news. In fact it was put to Derek that as he had shown his independence of the group and his own practical abilities, he would be more suited to living in a bed-sitter on his own than in a group setting; he was invited to the hostel and to make full use of all the facilities there, while retaining his independence in doing his own washing, etc. At this Derek finally perked up a little and . . . told us he "would be able to help in the hostel, and would be a great asset."

Thus when The Cherries was finally ready for the admission of residents the only remaining member of the group home group was Cathy.

*

CATHY

Year of birth 1938   I.Q. range 46–50
Parents – father: self-employed builder, stepmother: cook

Cathy went to an ordinary school until she was ten and then E.S.N. school until she was sixteen. Some physical handicap weakness of left arm and spastic leg. Stepmother ailing – finds Cathy too much at times. Therefore various periods of short-term care in hostels. Has a great desire for "freedom to plan her own life" and was therefore very anxious to move into the group home. No behaviour problems. Practical capabilities good, though sometimes limited by physical handicap. Employed in community just prior to group home admission, previously at training centre.

"Cathy seemed to be taking the whole thing in her stride and very much emerged as the sensible manager of the group, but although in some ways appearing in a slightly maternal role, I felt might remain fairly aloof from the rest of the group, very much concerned with making a home for herself and probably not getting as involved with the other members as we had first thought."

Possibly because of being slightly older than the others and having spent less time in residential care, Cathy's anxieties were not as great as those of the rest of the group. In fact she was at times more worried about the delay in moving to the group home than about what she would do when she got there. Her practical capabilities allied with a fairly stoic yet pleasant disposition, made her the one person sufficiently reliable to cope with the early troubles of the group home venture.

Because Cathy was the only one to move into The Cherries, it was thought desirable, for safety's sake, to move in a couple of social workers temporarily. This and the need to provide Cathy with transport to work (to be paid for by the Disablement Resettlement Office) meant a delay of about a month in finally moving Cathy to The Cherries. The delay caused Cathy further anxiety about never getting into the group home, and in addition she received the sad news of her elder brother's death. Towards the end of this period it was decided to take Cathy for a weekend. The original reason was described as "she would feel that the group home was a reality, and to relieve the hostel, who were finding it a strain having Cathy there talking about the group home non-stop".

The essentially pragmatic decision was to prove of fundamental importance to the later progress of the group home venture. The difficulties of conceptualizing life in an unknown environment have already been mentioned. Without spending time in the environment, during which mistakes and questions can arise and be dealt with, full commitment by a mentally handicapped person to such a change as is entailed by the move from dependent to independent living will rarely be made. For Cathy, however, the commitment was already intense, and the weekend merely acted as reinforcement. She moved into The Cherries on 8th December 1973.

Having only one admission to a twelve-bedded residential establishment by the opening date cannot be classed as a success for the admissions procedure. However, several lessons can be drawn from the events prior to Cathy's admission which might explain many of the problems encountered.

The first problem, and the most difficult to overcome, is the sheer uniqueness of the group home environment. The admissions policy outlined earlier was, and had to be, largely based on other forms of residential accommodation and thus emphasis was placed on practical rather than behavioural considerations. This would seem to be the result of the considerable, and well reported, underdevelopment of the abilities of the mentally handicapped in general, focusing attention on those who were, practically, capable of independent living. Subsequent experience would tend to indicate that social abilities, given some basic practical skills, may be a more useful criterion. These, of course, are much more difficult to measure since they involve the individual's effect on the group and its effect on him. At all events since their social abilities were not really assessed the early group were likely to come to grief in establishing stable relationships among themselves.

The group home's uniqueness also had an effect, as mentioned before, on the staff involved with the project. Uncertainty breeds suspicion and anxiety at all levels of human functioning, and it is likely that some people saw the group home as a possible replacement of, and therefore a threat to, hostels. Thus an attitude, although not reflected in

33

adverse action, may have built up, which contributed to the breakdown of the initial group. Once again it is difficult to see how this can be avoided with a new environment, particularly in this type of situation where a hostel acts as 'supplier' to a group home.

The second problem concerns the fact that the training period was also a time of assessment. This not only caused extra anxiety amongst the trainee group in that they felt 'on trial', but also was much more difficult at this time than subsequently when the home was available for 'on-site' assessment. In this context, the 'batch system' may have been a mistake, and only one or two people should move into a group home at a time. This, of course, goes against the economic maxim of full resource utilization at all times, but, as subsequent events will show, the long-term effect of such a policy is a more stable occupancy level, which, of course, leads to greater utilization. In any case, we shall also see emerging a case for group homes to house no more than three or four persons, so that the initial struggles to 'fill' The Cherries may be an isolated example brought about by the fact that the home was too large in the first place. This will be discussed more fully later. Without the omniscient power of hindsight, however, those associated with The Cherries were coming to terms with the problems facing their first resident.

CHAPTER IV

The first resident group

"You in your small corner and I in mine" English hymnal

For Cathy the first weekend in residence was, not unnaturally, something of a strain and it is scarcely surprising that her practical performance showed some signs of regression. After coping very well with budgeting and shopping during the weekend visit to the home

"... she had gone out shopping, first asking Stephanie (one of the social workers living in the home) how much money she should take with her. She had claimed to want to buy only half a dozen items and Stephanie suggested that one pound should cover it. However, Cathy had insisted on taking five pounds to be on the safe side and, in fact, had spent six pounds in the V.G. stores and bought more groceries than she could possibly carry."

Other problems were experienced with cooking a chicken for Sunday lunch, but even at this stage some signs of the effects of training were evident. "She had obviously planned ahead because she intended to eat the cold chicken on Monday." In addition, Cathy was determined to register with a new doctor, and this was felt to be a welcome sign of independence.

After a week or so, when she had settled into the home, her old capabilities began to return. During this time other potential residents had emerged.

*

MARY

Year of birth 1949   I.Q. range 81–85

Parents – father: lorry driver, mother: cleaner

Mary attended ordinary school until she was fifteen, but had various behavioural problems. Lived at home most of the time with occasional brief hostel visits prior to 1970. In hostel from 1970 onwards. On admission to hostel obtained job in community following employment at training centre. Thought to be capable of living alone in community. Moved into digs summer '73. Unable to cope. Thus considered for group home.

As Mary had proved extremely competent in the past, it was felt that she needed no training in practical matters, and so she was introduced to Cathy as soon as possible and given the opportunity of moving in if she wished. A meeting was arranged one evening at which Mary would be shown around the group home. It was thfought that the other potential residents might benefit from a visit and so the introduction of Mary was combined with a 'coffee party'. The visitors were Susan and Martin, from the original group home group, together with Barbara, Tina and Douglas who were being considered for future admission.

The conclusion earlier that there is no substitute for practical experience of a new environment was further borne out by this event.

"Everybody scattered all over the house, Susan, Barbara and Tina ran around looking in all the rooms and generally being nosey. We kept meeting and parting and there was general chaos for ten minutes while everybody raced round in and out of all the rooms."

After this initial burst of activity, the social workers and Cathy were bombarded with questions about the group home, which could of course be answered in a much more practical way in the surroundings of The Cherries. There was general enthusiasm for the home and the idea was mooted that a weekend visit should be made by the same group, after Mary had moved in. (The fact of Mary's admission had now been established.)

As Christmas was imminent, Mary did not move in for a couple of weeks, but on 29th December, together with Bobbie Moore the budgerigar, she took up residence. She seemed to settle in more easily than Cathy, perhaps because of her greater abilities, but also the presence of another resident must have helped.

As arranged at the coffee party, the first weekend visit took place shortly afterwards. Susan did not come with the weekend group because of a disciplinary matter at the hostel, but the other members were taken down on Friday evening by Linda. Mary and Cathy had already eaten and so the 'new group' prepared a meal for themselves. Although initially suspicious by the end of it the two had been invited to share the food which they did with evident enjoyment. Mary and Cathy were however very unsure of themselves and still had worries about having their new found freedoms restricted, or even being returned to the hostel. They therefore continued to be somewhat hostile towards the visitors and very possessive of their superior status and this seems to have been the only time that the actual and potential residents mixed during the weekend. Probably, faced with four visitors, the residents both felt somewhat overwhelmed, for this was, after all, supposed to be their own home.

A group meeting took place on the Sunday evening to discuss the events of the weekend and to see what lessons could be learned from it. The four visitors enjoyed talking about what they had done over the weekend and Tina and Barbara were especially pleased when the social workers praised their particular piece of initiative. They had been to a party in Watford on the Saturday evening and having been unable to find a taxi to take them home they had gone to the nearest police station for assistance. In the middle of this discussion, however, it was discovered that over £30 had been spent by the four over the weekend without their being able to account for it.

Some of the money had certainly been wasted on buying more food than was necessary for the weekend but helpful suggestions were made by the group which showed that they were aware of their own inadequacies in this matter. It was decided there and then to help 'weekenders' with their shopping on future occasions until they had learned the normal quantities and got some idea of prices since it was impossible to give them adequate facilities for training at the hostel. However, no one could explain what had happened to the majority of the money which the social workers never did manage to trace.

Overall, in fact, faced with the almost inexhaustible freedom after leading an organized and ordered life in the hostel the four visitors had become rather uninhibited in their enjoyment of this freedom. There were to be other occasions when Cherries residents got very drunk and stayed up all night, just because they had never been able to do it before. Once they suffered the consequences of hangovers, however, they began to realize that one didn't need to do things to excess to be able to enjoy them. Again, their behaviour is quite understandable: it is one of the normal reactions of any human when given a freedom that has long been denied to first go to extremes. In providing less institutionalized accommodation for mentally handicapped people it must be accepted that they will test their freedom to the full before taking to themselves the responsibility which had previously been 'somebody else's'.

As a means of assessment, however, the weekend had proved a great success and the selection committee decided that further weekends should be planned. As a result of the lessons learned from the first weekend the next few visits proved much more successful, mainly because the social workers put extra effort into helping with shopping and budgeting, and because the weekenders soon realized the need to show responsibility if they were to be allowed to move in.

At the end of January it was decided that both Martin and Tina were ready for such a move. Martin had recovered from his asthma, and the weekend visits had allayed his worries about the group home. In addition, though he was certainly not the most competent of people under consideration for The Cherries, it was felt that Cathy and Mary were sufficiently settled to be able to help him.

The whole group were told of the admission decisions at a meeting the following week.

"Susan and Douglas had no difficulty in accepting our decision not to let them move in at once, but Barbara seemed very put out, even though I explained to her that we were allowing Martin and Tina to go first because they had been in the hostel for such a long time."

37

Decisions on selection were, of course, being continually reviewed, and it might be useful to consider why Susan, Barbara and Douglas were not thought suitable at this stage.

Susan's history has already been given, and the reasons for her non-admission at this point were no different from hitherto. She was still not sure in her own mind about moving in, and still displayed considerable immaturity and anxiety during the weekend visits, which upset the group. In particular, she showed extreme dependence on the social worker whenever she was around, and would, therefore, probably be a considerable drain on the supportive resources of the group. The same would apply to Douglas.

*

DOUGLAS

Year of birth 1944   I.Q. range 81–85

Parents – father: unknown, mother: retired housekeeper

Lived at home, working in community until 1972 when moved into hostel, transferred to hospital when hostel closed. On favourable report of psychiatrist was transferred to a new hostel although reported as being very dependent on a secure place and very reluctant to move on when settled. Also under extensive medication.

Although in the hostel at the time of the initial group selection, Douglas's heavy medication and general lethargy did not recommend him as a candidate, despite his having the necessary practical qualifications. However, he had improved somewhat and thus was included in the new group. He himself had expressed reservations about the move, and it was felt that he should not be pushed too hard, especially as the resident group were not yet stable enough to provide support. He, like Susan, remained a long term prospect.

Barbara's situation was slightly different.

*

BARBARA

Year of birth 1942   I.Q. range 51–55

Parents: Divorced – little contact

From age of 12 lived in hospital, though short period in hostel later on. Illegitimate child born while Barbara in hospital, now in care. Small contribution is necessary for child. Thought suitable for group living. Moved into hostel for preparation.

Barbara had only just moved to the hostel from hospital, and still had problems coping with frustration and her temper, although this seemed

38

to be under greater control at the hostel. She was expected to move in fairly soon, but a slightly longer period of assessment was felt to be necessary.

A further weekend had already been agreed upon and it was suggested that Martin and Tina should move in on the Saturday following their next visit. The weekend went very smoothly and thus there was nothing to prevent Martin and Tina moving in on 9th February.

Tina was much more competent than Martin and was very enthusiastic about moving in and being independent, but with her ideas of independence she quickly fell foul of the others.

*

TINA

Year of birth 1952   I.Q. range 81–85

Parents – father: engineer, mother: died when Tina was 8

Lived with grandmother as a child, ordinary school until 1961 then residential special school until 1969. Temper tantrums and destructiveness, at home only. Moved to hostel on leaving school, also had a job in community. Was unhappy in hostel away from her father. Transferred in 1971 to hostel closer to home. Some slight spasticity.

Tina moved in at the same time as Martin but before she had been at The Cherries very long she stopped paying her rent regularly. This was because she was staying at home all day to 'do her own thing' instead of going to work. Naturally enough the others were somewhat annoyed at having to pay rent and go to work when Tina was having to do neither and so they started voicing their grievances to the social workers, who were already concerned about Tina's behaviour.

Tina herself reverted to tantrums and aggressive behaviour when the matter was first raised, and, as it became clear that the group disapproved of her behaviour, she started to remove herself more and more from group meetings. This naturally enabled the remaining residents to express their feelings more openly than they would have done in her presence. Finally, the social worker, as a result of group pressure, felt it necessary, after continuous general warnings, to give Tina a specific deadline by which to pay the rent. She was informed that, if she did not meet it, she would be sent back to the hostel. This seemed to have some effect and shortly afterwards Tina paid a week's rent and seemed to be attempting to re-establish herself in her job. Thus the group settled down again to a peaceful if slightly uneasy existence.

The independent Cathy proceeded, with assistance from the social worker on such matters as sick notes etc., to survive comfortably in the group home. Although an active member of the group, taking part in discussions and doing her share of the housework, she tended to remain aloof from any friction. Martin was, to some extent, mothered by the other members of the group because of his lower capabilities, though at times his behaviour provoked annoyance. He had never taken a major role in discussions and did not assume one now. Mary and Tina were both coping very well with their own lives at the group home, although friction often arose when the four combined, especially during the discussion at group meetings. This was seen to be a leadership clash, though of a relatively minor nature.

Despite such problems among the resident four they still tended to combine when faced with 'weekenders'. Neither group however was really prepared to say what they felt in front of the others. After one weekend, for example, the group home group complained that they (the weekenders) "do not clean up after themselves – do not change sheets – leave the beds dirty and do not pull their weight". They also seemed concerned about Barbara's drinking, saying that once she had come home drunk, and fallen asleep on the T.V. lounge floor. Susan's worrying, and her tendency to get up during the night, was also a cause of friction. For their part, the weekend group, at a separate meeting, complained that "the group living there do not make them welcome when they go down for weekends. They told me that the group do not own the home, that they have as much right to be there as the people living there and they should be more welcoming."

By putting opposite points of view at the meetings, the social worker tried to persuade both groups to modify their views somewhat to prevent further complaint. This was reasonably successful, but attempts to get the groups to meet together to discuss their problems failed in the face of people's refusal to speak openly.

It is worth noting here that the time span between significant events was becoming greater. During the initial training period, and virtually until Martin and Tina moved into the home, intervention of some sort by the social worker, or one of the hostel staff, whether merely for a chat, or for more practical purposes, had occurred almost daily. Now, as the weekends became slightly more routine, though they still had to be organized, direct social work activity seems to have decreased until it centred around the weekend. However, this could be considered as a case of no, or less, news being good news, since the everyday life of the residents went quietly by, thus beginning to meet one of the major objectives of The Cherries.

A considerable improvement had, therefore, taken place in the direction of the group home project. Although there were still only four residents in occupation five months after Cathy had moved in, an important pattern had been established which was to continue into the future. The fundamental points of this pattern were, first, the weekend visits by potential residents and, second, group meetings at which anxieties and fears could be discussed and, in the main, allayed. This was essentially a formalization of a policy that had come about by experimentation, and had been observed to work in practice. It should be pointed out, however, that the group were still not living totally independently, since one of the social workers, who moved in at the same time as Cathy, was still resident, although taking no part, deliberately, in group proceedings. She was due to move out at the end of May, and that month was to see a number of other significant changes.

The hostel residents were going on their annual holiday in May, and at the first group meeting of the month it was suggested that Barbara and Susan should move in after the holiday. This meeting preceded a weekend visit, and a new member was to be added to the visiting group. This was Richard, who was the person who had been upset by the separation of the group home group in the early days. Of the regular visiting group, Douglas was missing, and Derek was included.

*

RICHARD

Year of birth 1942   I.Q. range 66–70

Parents – father: general labourer, stepmother: cleaner

Ordinary schools for first five years of schooling. Then residential special school until aged 16. At school said to have temper tantrums and erratic behaviour. Is epileptic but well controlled. Only a few fits per year. On leaving school, moved to hospital. Stayed for eleven years till 1969 when moved to hostel. Thought capable of working in the community if his slowness could be tolerated. Currently attends A.T.C. Very institutionalized on entry to hostel. Violent behaviour much diminished since early 1960's although reputation for violence remained.

The resident group were aware of the imminent departure of Stephanie, the resident social worker, and thus they were facing three problems, as they saw it, all at once, i.e. the prospect of complete independence for the first time, the responsibility for two new members, one with a reputation for drunkenness and the other who had already shown her need for attention and support, together with the immediate worry of a new weekend visitor who had a reputation, although more among residents than staff, for violent behaviour. It is scarcely surprising that these worries came to a head, which they did during the ensuing weekend.

Three incidents occurred, which were more symptomatic of the general problems and worries, than particular to that one weekend. On the Sunday evening a meeting of the hostel staff and social worker attached to the group home took place, concerning events that had occurred over the weekend.

"Several things had happened that day and they (the hostel staff) were all very concerned.

41

Tina had telephoned them and complained that the evening before Barbara had come in drunk and had been sick. She had collapsed in the television room and they had not been able to wake her. Tina and Susan had, therefore, sat down on the stairs outside the television room. Martin, who had Desmond to stay that weekend, had emerged from his room in his pyjamas, he had been going to the loo but stopped on the landing. Tina had told him to put his dressing gown on as his pyjamas were hardly covering him. Martin had then swung his leg over the banisters revealing all and shocking Tina. Mary had been to the hostel and had been asked what had happened the night before. She had said little but finally revealed that people had been throwing papers and rubbish out of the window at the group which had been playing at the working men's club."

The result of these events was, in fact, more beneficial than could be envisaged from the nature of the incidents. A meeting was arranged, of all the people concerned, for the following evening at the group home. The social worker concerned with the group

". . . felt that this would be very helpful because in the past I have liaised with Malcolm (the hostel warden), found out what was being said by each group but been totally unable without breaking confidences to force the group to confront each other about these issues. I have tried such things as holding separate groups to find out how each group feels about the other and then bringing them together and bringing up things or giving them openings to bring things up themselves, but to no avail. I felt that if the hostel staff were prepared to bring up in the big group, things that had been said to them possibly in confidence, this would be an excellent way of getting things out into the open and discussing them. I agreed that what had been said about Martin was serious enough to warrant this kind of treatment in the group setting."

What followed was exceedingly painful but it at last brought out not only the background to the incidents mentioned, but also some of the general problems that the group faced. As this represents something of a watershed in the development of the group home the diary will be quoted at length. The meeting was attended by: three members of the hostel staff, Malcolm, Alfred and Joe; the group home social worker; the four residents, Mary, Cathy, Martin and Tina; and the visitors of the weekend, Barbara, Susan, Richard and Douglas.

All those from the hostel arrived at the group home, and a circle of chairs was set up for the ensuing meeting.

"I then opened the meeting saying that things that had been said over the weekend at the hostel which were of a serious nature and which I felt needed to be brought out in the open. I said that I brought down the hostel staff as they wished to bring up things that had been said to them. I then threw the meeting back to the hostel staff to say what they wanted.

We started with what Tina had reported and broke this down into two issues. 1. Barbara's drunkenness. 2. Martin's exposing himself. We went over in detail what had happened to Barbara and we learned that she tends to drink too much. This only occurs however on a Saturday night, she comes back and is sick or falls onto the television room floor. I pointed out that we had discussed this all before and I had told them they could leave her there or contact the duty

42

officer. I stressed that duty is a 24 hour business and that if there is any emergency they can get somebody at any time of the day or night and that that is what we were there for. When we had talked about Barbara's behaviour, Tina admitted that she had been more worried about Barbara than cross and, in fact, I felt that the group is able to tolerate Barbara's drunkenness although I feel that they are a little apprehensive at the fact that Barbara is due to move in. In fact I felt that much of the disturbance this weekend was caused by all the changes and the reflection of their anxieties at having Barbara who has a reputation for violence, Susan who needs a lot of mothering, and when they are about to lose Stephanie from the home.

We then went on to talk about Martin's behaviour. Tina described in detail what had happened and how upset she had been. We questioned Martin about this and it was clear that he had been angry with Tina for telling him off about not wearing a dressing gown and that he had had one or two drinks too. As he is extremely inarticulate he could not put into words what he had been feeling and what motivated his behaviour.

Once the group got started about Martin's behaviour they went on and on at great length about what he does. I felt very anxious for him at this point as he seemed to be receiving little support from anybody and Mary and Tina in particular backed up by Barbara and Susan, were complaining about his silly behaviour, which they say is getting The Cherries a bad name. We talked as we had in the past about his behaviour in the pub when he had got himself thrown out because he swore and how he dresses up in his anorak looking as silly as possible and behaves in such a way that children laugh at him in the street and call him names. I had had a word with Douglas and Martin about this previously and he had complained to me about children shouting after him and calling him a spastic. I had then pointed out that he could have provoked this himself but felt I had failed to get him to see this. I felt that Martin was being scapegoated for the stigma which is bound to be attached to a place like The Cherries and at one point Malcolm pointed out that this is a fact of life for the mentally handicapped and that they were going to have to learn to live with it and not blame Martin. I got quite angry with them at one point, feeling that they were only concerned about the name they are getting and have no motivation to help Martin to overcome his difficulties. I felt too that once Martin is accused of silly behaviour he hides behind a defence of further silliness which perpetuates and aggravates the problem. It struck me at this point that it would be helpful for Martin to have a male social worker to talk these things over with as he is the only male in the home with a lot of women around. I had also learned that at the hostel the staff used to give him the odd cuddle and he probably misses this physical contact. I then went on to ask them about all the mess that I understood Stephanie had found on Sunday morning after they had been throwing rubbish out of the windows. Richard and Cathy had not been present at this but I understood that Tina, Barbara and Susan and all the others had done this. I pointed out to them that they could hardly blame Martin for bringing stigma to the place if they were going to behave like this. I was angry with them that Stephanie had had to clear up the mess and also annoyed that some of the things thrown outside could have caused punctures if cars had driven over them. I pointed all this out and they all said they realized the folly of their ways and would reform. Up till now the group leadership had gone from me initially to Malcolm on behalf of the hostel staff to Tina who was the centre of attention because of her complaint.

Attention was now focused on Derek. I was pleased that we had finally forced him to come to a meeting as he manages to opt out successfully from any meeting I hold when he can choose whether he is there or not, and in fact I feel the resource of a group home is totally wasted on him. It appeared that Mary had rung the hostel early that morning to say that Derek had ordered Susan to bring his case back but that it was impossible for Susan to manage this on the bus. Mary also said that Derek was always ordering people around. Susan actually managed, with Malcolm's support to steel herself to complain about Derek's tyranny and Derek had accused Mary in a fit of temper at the hostel of always poking her nose into things. We now all defended Mary pointing out to Derek that as he took no part in the group and was absent for most of every weekend he spends there, he could not possibly know whether Mary poked her nose into things or not and that he was not around to have her nose poked into his affairs anyway. This was all a bit too subtle for Derek: he got very flustered, denied everything and fantasized as he usually does. It was not a very constructive discussion with Derek and I did not feel we had made any progress or that he would change in the future. However there was a vast amount of group pressure put on him to change from his bullying ways.

At the end of the meeting we said that we would be doing this more often and it was agreed that it was a good thing to have everything out into the open. During this discussion Cathy and Richard, who I feel were not particularly involved in what had been going on over the weekend, took a back seat only endorsing things that were said. Susan was very involved non verbally but too timid to say very much except when she had someone to follow. Derek as usual opted out except when he was dragged into the discussion and reacted belligerently with his usual somewhat paranoid aggressive behaviour. Mary was less dominant than usual being curbed by the presence of the hostel staff who have had to dominate her in the past. Tina and Barbara were quite forthcoming and emerged as strong characters when they want to be. Martin did his best to keep up with the conversation although I feel he is at a considerable drawback because of his low I.Q. I felt it was significant that Susan sat on Malcolm's right, Derek sat on my left and Richard also sat by me. Malcolm, Mary and myself were spaced at equal distances from each other round the group forming a triangle as it were. Alfred and Joe sat between Malcolm and Mary and the permanent residents at the group home seemed to be sitting nearer me."

It is probable that something like this was necessary to clear the air, and at last both potential and actual residents had been forced to express their worries in each other's presence. It had been agreed by the staff previously, and, as reported above, endorsed by the meeting, that joint meetings like these should be established after each visiting weekend, i.e. fortnightly. As mentioned in the diary, separate group meetings of visitors and residents had brought out some problems, but the problems of communication between the two were relieved by such a joint discussion. Some of the characters of both groups can be seen more clearly from the description of the meeting. The leadership struggle between Tina and Mary continued, but Barbara also began to develop as a strong character in her own right. Derek's unsuitability for the group was fully exposed at last, by the group itself as much as by the social worker. Susan remained easily led and did not contribute much, while Martin struggled to keep up, at times leaving himself open to the hostility of the group, as a 'payment' for the support they gave him. Cathy remained apart and does not seem to have been at all involved, but had found a 'kindred spirit' in Richard who was also fairly quiet and independent.

The three worries of the group home residents were thus diminished. Barbara's moving in, following the general discussion, was seen as less of a problem, although the difficulty with Susan remained. Richard had fitted in well, in as much as he had been adopted by Cathy, and thus had remained apart from all but her. The social worker was still due to leave, but now the group felt able to discuss their anxieties. At a later group meeting . . .

". . . I then talked to them about Stephanie's leaving as I know they are worried and going to miss her. We discussed their feelings of anxiety at not having a social worker living there and their ambivalence about the dependence, independence bit. Mary said that if we had a residential social worker when Susan moved in she would always be round plaguing her and that she felt this was a bad thing. I said that if Susan behaved in this way this meant that the rest of them would get the full force of Susan's behaviour. They all however seemed capable of coping with it from what they said."

In general, the traumatic experience of the Monday meeting seemed to have enabled the resident group to 'turn the corner'.

"I went down for the usual group meeting with Mary, Tina, Cathy and Martin. There seemed to be a reluctance to refer to Monday's meeting but I insisted on bringing this up and asking how they felt about it now. They all agreed that it had been a good thing, if painful at the time, and I felt that they were more at ease with each other than before Monday."

The description of, and comments on, events to date may have presented a picture of life in the group home which is not entirely accurate. This is because the development of the group, both residents and visitors, has tended to be highlighted by the problems experienced and the reactions to them, and thus, in describing their development, emphasis has been placed on these problems. This may have given the impression that the group home venture was failing, or at least struggling against heavy odds. In fact the reverse was true, but this is only demonstrated by the sheer fact of the group's continued existence, and the residents' increased ability to cope with their own problems and develop mutually satisfying relationships. Everyday events tend to go unnoticed even though they might herald a new development in group living, whereas crises though infrequent have to be solved.

The daily routine of the residents when the 'weekenders' were not there passed much as any normal working person's. The four got up, breakfasted, and went their separate ways to work. Cathy and Mary had taxis provided, Cathy because of her spasticity, and Mary because of the distance involved and the lack of public transport. Tina, with only a short distance to travel, took the bus, and Martin cycled to work. Two of the group, Cathy and Tina, had factory jobs, Mary worked in a laundry and Martin in a furniture store warehouse. Although the employers had good contacts with the Social Services Department, the handicapped were not given special treatment.

The four returned home at different times and generally cooked their meals separately. Evening and weekend entertainment varied in much the same way as most people's. Watching television, or a visit to the pub were fairly regular activities, but these were interspersed with a variety of other things, e.g. visits to and from relatives and friends.

At 'visiting' weekends, of course, this routine was broken by the introduction of new people, and during these weekends the social workers were much more in evidence. These times apart, the only direct social work activity with the residents was the Monday evening meeting, although occasional visits took place to deal with specific incidents, e.g. to let in the meter reader.

Thus, the pattern of unobtrusive daily living that was to continue as the group developed began to be established. In addition, one or two events were noted in the diary, which show how far the group had come from the early days. It should, of course, be remembered that only five months had passed since Cathy moved in.

"I learned from Cathy that she had had trouble not having an alarm clock and had got up at half past two in the morning, thinking it was time to go to work. This was not the first time this had happened and I was concerned about this. Everybody, however, seemed very tolerant of Cathy's behaviour and they were not complaining about it. Mary had now lent Cathy her alarm clock so that she would be able to get up at the right time in the morning and then wake Mary. I was pleased that they had managed to sort this out in a friendly manner, as previously I had observed a lot of antagonism towards Cathy."

This sort of cooperation in overcoming the trivial problems of everyday life, which had taken place without prompting, illustrates how far the residents had progressed in becoming a group, taking joint responsibility for decisions. It should not be forgotten, as well, that to many people the sheer fact of a group of mentally handicapped adults living in an unsupervised situation is an amazing achievement. To those involved in the subject, this will not be such a shock, since the practical capabilities of the mentally handicapped, given training, have been demonstrated in several studies[50,51]. However, even among those working with the mentally handicapped, the idea of unsupervised group living is thought of as something of an idealistic dream. By their performance of the trivial everyday tasks, the group were beginning to make that dream a reality.

CHAPTER V

Movements in and out

"These simple little rules and few" H. Belloc – *The Python*

A few weeks after the eventful weekend, the residents of the hostel went on holiday abroad. Martin went with them, leaving the three women, Cathy, Mary and Tina, alone in the home. It was planned that Susan and Barbara would move in the first weekend after they returned from the holiday, although there was still some anxiety on the part of the residents about Susan, and a group meeting was arranged to discuss her particular problems before she finally moved in.

With the holiday over, the position had altered slightly. Susan had once again decided that she did not wish to move into the group home. The decision had come after a row on holiday, but it was felt that this was, again, the result of Susan building up her worries. The row was over Susan wanting to change rooms and stop sharing with Barbara, and caused Susan to claim that she always got blamed for everything and did not want to move into the group home. While this meant that Barbara could move in on her own, thus relieving some of the fears of the residents, it did not overcome the problem of Susan ever making a decision to move in. Because she was so easily led it was felt undesirable to push her one way or the other. The resident group were beginning to become impatient with Susan's indecision as shown when the matter was discussed at a group meeting.

"I said that I felt and had said to Susan that evening that she should do exactly what she wanted to do, with no pressure from anyone being put on her. I then said I thought that possibly Susan would still carry on with the weekends. Mary then said she did not see why Susan should block up weekends when she might never get round to moving into the group home. I pointed out to Mary that there were loads of beds in the group home and Susan was not blocking a place but I saw her point that if we got to the point that there was only one bed, we would have to give someone else preference if Susan had still not taken the plunge. However, I said we would leave it to Susan to decide whether she wished to move in or not and whether she wished to have weekends and would not need to give her an ultimatum for a long time yet."

At this same meeting Derek was finally excluded from weekend visits. This had been discussed with the group before who felt that he was unsuitable, mainly because of his lack of interest in the group and his tendency to spend the majority of his time at the hostel even when staying at The Cherries for weekends.

Barbara moved in on 7th June with no major problems. She, like Cathy, and, in fact, all new residents, regressed slightly on moving in, but again as with all residents this did not last long. The resident group now contained Cathy, Mary, Tina, Martin and Barbara with the only remaining weekenders being Richard, Susan and Douglas, although Douglas was being reviewed because of some strange behaviour on holiday. For the next two months there occurred one of those periods of slow development which contained little in the way of remarkable incidents, but added greatly to the group's stability. Again the sheer fact of five mentally handicapped people living in the community, and coping with everyday life, should be noted.

Towards the end of this period, however, Tina's behaviour was, once again, beginning to cause concern.

"Mary, Cathy, Barbara and Martin were present for the meeting all extremely agitated about Tina. According to Martin, Tina had got up early, had put some clothes in Barbara's bag and had told him she wasn't going to work. They thought she would be at her grandmother's.

The discussion continued and the group brought up many grudges mainly about the fact that Tina was not bothering to work so why should they. Barbara accused her of taking some of her clothes without permission and Mary said she had been borrowing money from her tin. Martin had lost his bank book the previous Saturday and they had searched his room thoroughly; after mentioning to Tina that they had filled in a form for a lost book, it has reappeared. Linda (one of the social workers) and I promised to contact her employer and check whether she had been to work and if not, we would take positive action such as moving Tina out of The Cherries. They agreed this was the best treatment for Tina."

Since the early days of her residence Tina has only worked spasmodically and, as already mentioned, this did not meet with approval of the group. She had survived one ultimatum, and seemed to be making progress, although by the competition between her and Mary for leadership of the group, harmony was not always maintained. Her temper, though not often displayed, caused reluctance in the group to discuss her poor employment record in her presence. Undoubtedly, however, it was her failure to fit into the norms of the group regarding working and paying rent which caused them to press for her removal. Following the group meeting quoted above, another ultimatum was issued by the social worker.

"I went round The Cherries and the doors were locked and Tina did not answer the door bell, so I let myself in and went up to Tina's room. She was extremely nervous and stood at the window with her back to me shouting that she was tired of Slough and would not discuss what was worrying her. I explained that her employers were holding her job until Wednesday and if she decided not to take it, she would have to leave The Cherries and move back to the hostel. With a final thought that she didn't care about anyone but herself, Tina stormed out of the room.

I returned to The Cherries about 5 p.m. to be greeted very apologetically by Tina who made me some tea and was very anxious that I wouldn't be upset by her earlier remarks. I promised to pick her up at 7.30 a.m. on Wednesday 14th August to take her to work and she could then work out which bus to get home in the evening."

Despite her returning to work for one day on that Wednesday, it was apparent within one week that 'the only way to make Tina go out to work was to move her to the hostel'. This move occurred, under protest from Tina, on 22nd August.

In some senses Tina had acted as a catalyst in formulating the group's attitude on non-working and payment of rent. Their opinions had been evident in their reactions to Tina's earlier behaviour and now, at the instigation of the social worker, a formal statement of policy was agreed.

"Mary suggested two weeks was the limit of unemployment unless a sick note was produced, also a two weeks limit should be put for non-payment of rent, although Mary suggested that if they were only able to pay part of it this should be accepted. The others agreed, although Barbara thought one week should be long enough to find a job as you could spend all day looking. The final decision was:
    1. two weeks was the limit for unemployment unless they were off sick.
    2. two weeks was the limit for non-payment of rent.
If these conditions were not observed, the person involved must leave The Cherries". (NB 'Employment', of course, included the Adult Training Centre)

As well as this instance of acting in concert against Tina, the resident group were showing in other ways signs of their independence of supportive staff.

The least surprising of these came from Cathy, since her determination and self-reliance had already been demonstrated. Now she managed to book and arrange a coach trip for herself. The decision to do this had been entirely her own, and she apparently spent a very enjoyable week seeing some of the sights of Scotland. Once again a look back to Cathy's history will show that, even for her, this was no mean feat.

Other incidents show the residents acting as a group and collectively showing their increasing maturity.

An official from a Social Services Department in the North of England was invited to a group meeting, because he was hoping to set up a group home in his area, and wanted to discover the residents' impressions of group home living. The significant fact about this visit was the reaction of the group to a remark by the visitor: "He said that there was very little money, but that there was a great need for some kind of hostel or group home, and he wanted to find out what the best facility would be." The residents were strongly in favour of the idea of group homes, although some discussion focused on the ideal size of such a home.

49

"We started discussing the pros and cons of large groups and council house sized groups and I (the social worker) said that I felt it would be easier to run a small group of three or four than to find twelve people who could all fit in together in a larger building. They all seemed to feel that this was true and started discussing with the visitor how he could get hold of a council house, and how he could divide up the bedrooms to get three, four, five or even six people in if he wanted to. Then Mary dominated the discussion for quite a long time, telling the visitor all about fund raising and describing in detail exactly what they had done at the hostel. She explained how every trainee had played their part, and then described how pubs collected money in bottles. She then went on to say that she would have a fund raising event, such as a dance, here and send him the money."

About two months later ten pounds was sent to aid in the visitor's group home project. This had been raised by a raffle held at a party organized by the group home residents and attended by guests invited by them: hostel members, staff of the Social Services Department and other friends from elsewhere.

Another event shows independence, almost amounting to cunning, on the part of the group. Whilst Mary was on holiday, Martin, at a group meeting, "announced that they wanted to have a dog."

"Cathy backed up Martin's request, saying that they wanted to know if they could have our full permission to keep a dog there. We discussed it with them and I said that originally, we had decided that no-one would have a dog and that I would have to check back at the office with the boss to find out whether it would be allowed. It then transpired that Mary's friend's dog had had puppies and that one of these had been suggested. Barbara announced that they were going to call it Sandy, whatever it was. We discussed the pros and cons of having a puppy or a dog that had been in a home and Christine (the other social worker) told them that puppies always wanted to chew and if they are shut up during the day, tend to get into everything and chew things to pieces. I said that as this was the case with puppies I was sure that we would only be allowed to have an older dog. I turned to Martin, saying that as his father ran a kennels and knew all about dogs, we really ought to use this and ask his advice on it. Martin said that whenever he had mentioned it to his father, he had told him that he must discuss it with me and that they had had a row and Martin had slammed down the phone. I suggested that perhaps Christine or I could ring and that we could find out whether it was all right for a dog to be cooped up all day in the house and generally ask his advice about the matter. They pointed out that they looked after the rabbit well and were quite capable and I felt that they were, in fact."

After this discussion, which had left the matter subject to approval, the social workers were met with a 'fait accompli' on their next visit: "when we arrived we found there was a little puppy there." At first the reaction was to allow them to keep it.

"We told them that we had not, in fact, got permission for them to have a puppy, but that as it was their own home and they were allowed to do as they would in their own home, we supposed that they could keep it, but we must be very careful to make sure that it got sufficient exercise, and did not cause any damage to the place. Mary was full of bright ideas for training and seemed to know what she was talking about."

Unfortunately, this particular episode did not end happily as the group were unable to look after the dog during the day when they were at work and being a puppy it did make quite a considerable mess in the home. This resulted in the dog being removed after a couple of months following a decision by The Cherries committee who were still the arbiters of policy in the home. However, the point of this example is not concerned with the issue of whether a dog should be kept or not, but that the residents had acted independently in acquiring the animal, and in their attempts to look after it.

On being told of a camping holiday which Christine had taken, the group expressed a desire to have one of their own. The point illustrated by the camping weekend that followed is not so much that it occurred but that the group were able to relate the experience of another to their own ideas of an enjoyable event and to participate in planning one for themselves, something they had previously been unable to do. Thus, although the weekend was 'organized' and the social workers went along it was fundamentally a group home holiday. Another interesting point was that the resident group invited two of the weekenders to join their holiday: Richard, who was by now a regular weekender, and Doreen, who had started visiting. (Susan and Douglas had by now become intermittent visitors and were not invited.) Despite inclement weather, the weekend passed quite happily and similar group holidays were talked of enthusiastically. These incidents illustrate the gradual stability being induced into the resident group, and this is further borne out when consideration was given to the next resident, Richard.

Following the camping weekend Richard moved in on 6th October. From the early days of his connection with the group home, Richard had tended to associate more with Cathy than with the others. For example the diary records a reaction to his first weekend.

"This led on to weekends and I asked how Richard had got on as they had been so apprehensive about his visiting. Cathy was forthcoming about this, telling me warmly that he had enjoyed himself and she and he had done various things together. I felt that she had very much appreciated his visit to the group home and that the companionship had been good for her. They all seem to have liked Richard's company and had told me that he had been well behaved, and not lost his temper. This fitted in with what I had seen of Richard and I was pleased about this."

Over the subsequent weekends, prior to his taking up residence, Richard and Cathy continued to do things together, and it was, therefore, no surprise when, at a group meeting, shortly after the move, it was learnt that they were sharing a room. It was equally unsurprising to learn that there was no physical relationship involved, but merely an extension of the friendship they had developed. It was felt that, apart

51

from ensuring that adequate sex education was given, no attempt should be made to dictate the form of their relationship. They had combined their lives to the extent of cooking and shopping together, with jointly agreed menus being bought and cooked by Cathy.

The relationship did however bring into the open a moral question that had hitherto been dormant, namely, the fact that the group home was a mixed sex establishment and that association between the sexes was permitted. The moral implications obviously depend on the form the association takes, but it was practically inevitable that something like the relationship between Richard and Cathy would arise. It is even possible that a more physical relationship could occur. Reaction to this must depend, to some extent, on reaction to group living in general, not just among the mentally handicapped. Those who oppose any unsupervised mixing of sexes in residential accommodation will naturally disagree with the group home idea. However, even amongst those who approve of 'mixing' for 'normal' people, there are those who find the idea objectionable in the context of the mentally handicapped. It is difficult in our opinion to see the distinction between the rights of the handicapped to associate with members of the opposite sex, and any other rights they possess, e.g. to vote, providing that adequate precautions are taken to avoid the possible genetic problems involved. Thus if effective sex education is provided as it was for the group home residents, the choice is between any rights of independent functioning of the handicapped, or none. This must remain a question of moral attitude, but to be specific, the relationship between Cathy and Richard seemed to be of great benefit to them, and was welcomed by all those connected with the group home as a sign of the maturity and independence that the group had achieved.

Doreen was now the only regular weekend visitor.

*

DOREEN

Year of birth 1936   I.Q. range 55–60 (earlier tests gave range 81–85)
Parents – father: plater, mother: part-time domestic
Ordinary schools till aged 8 then various special schools. Hospital from age 15 till 1970 with two brief discharges in 1962 and 1965 to lodgings in community. These not successful. Early epilepsy deemed hysterical. No fits for sometime. Long history of behaviour disturbance with occasional spontaneous aggression. Still some aggression but greater stability following move to hostel in 1970. Practical abilities entirely adequate.

Doreen had suffered from falling between a number of classificatory stools. Those who like to define mental handicap by I.Q. would not, on the basis of her earlier tests, put her in that category, but on the other hand, the degree of her behaviour disturbance did not really warrant the label mental illness. As in many cases this lack of an accepted 'label' had meant that Doreen had never really received care suitable to her total needs. At this time she was dealt with under the aegis of the mental handicap services and, being reasonably competent, she had been considered for admission to the group home and thus began weekend visits.

Whilst at The Cherries she had renewed her friendship with Barbara whom she had known from hospital days, but being rather inarticulate her participation in group meetings was rather limited:

"Doreen did not join in very much though she seemed to take part in the group with her eyes."

Having successfully taken her place as a weekender the only problem to be solved before she could be admitted was her aggressive behaviour. This aggression had not been in evidence during the period of her weekend visits and continued stability during these visits and at the hostel removed all further obstacles to her admission. She was therefore moved in to The Cherries at the end of November.

CHAPTER VI

A period of stability

"not with a bang, but a whimper" T. S. Eliot – *The Hollow Men*

The group of six residents created by Doreen's arrival achieved something of an established air fairly quickly, and as the Christmas of 1976 approached the customary festivities were being planned. Once again the most striking thing about these plans was their normality. Things and people were 'organized' – who would do what; buying food and drink, arranging visits; presents – all the normal rush and bustle of Christmas. The traditional Christmas family contact was there too, with most people visiting relatives during the holiday period, but the feeling that The Cherries was now a real home meant that only Mary was prepared to forgo the group celebration on Christmas Day itself.

Christmas continued to dominate the talk at group meetings on into the new year, with residents anxious to describe their enjoyable experiences to the social workers. This tended to make other matters less important but the process of introducing individuals by weekend visits continued. The three major candidates at this point were Douglas who had been kept as a long term prospect and two newcomers, Christopher and Sally.

*

CHRISTOPHER

Year of birth 1954   I.Q. range: unknown

Parents – father: labourer, mother: housewife

One of five children born to mentally handicapped parents. All children mentally handicapped and Christopher the brightest. Went to special school until 16. Several jobs on leaving school but dismissed from these "due to slowness". A nervous and excitable person. Christopher, whilst fond of his parents, could not cope with their instability and was thus moved to hostel. Because he was capable and fairly articulate, considered for the group home.

*

SALLY

Year of birth 1956   I.Q. range 56–60

Parents – father: window cleaner, stepmother: occupation unknown

At home attending ESN school until 16. Moved into hostel soon after leaving school because of home problems. Very quiet and shy with strangers, but bright and cheerful among friends. Suffers from epilepsy with occasional hysterical attacks. Works at Adult Training Centre.

The only other possible candidate for admission at that stage was Susan, but she was not one of the current visitors since her own continuing nervousness about The Cherries caused her to be regarded by the social workers as a long term prospect rather than an immediate one.

All three of the weekenders were established hostel residents and thus knew The Cherries group fairly well. Christopher was the most competent of the three, intellectually as well as practically, but his personality began to cause some friction. His home background had instilled something of a sense of inadequacy in Christopher, for which he tended to compensate by taking an independent and aggressive line in the group home. This in its turn provoked some hostile reactions from the group, mainly in the form of leaving Christopher out of certain group activities, which of course reinforced his feelings of rejection. His answer to the situation was to increase his façade of independence to the extent of not only presenting a negative attitude to any proposed group activity, but also trying to avoid those parts of weekend visits used for training purposes, e.g. shopping expeditions with the social workers. In group meetings he used his high verbal capability to challenge Mary's leadership of the group, but if he was unsuccessful he tended to withdraw and take no further part in the proceedings. This was normally the case since Mary had, of course, the backing of the resident group, as well as her own ability to dominate. Thus, for example, the social worker reports on one meeting "Mary's mood was very aggressive but then reasonable at the end. The rest seemed to follow her mood though the leadership came from Christopher, Christine (the other social worker) and myself." Whereas on another "Christopher tried to dominate and was squashed or ignored by them". By the end of January relations between Christopher and the group seemed to be worsening. This is shown, for example, by a group meeting soon afterwards where:

"The holiday was discussed. Christine had brought a map of North Devon and various brochures. Mary was adamant that a holiday had to be a rest and that we could not therefore go camping because this was too much like hard work. . . . Christopher was ambivalent about whether he wanted to come or not. This may have been because he could not afford it, or because he tried to play hard to get because he has feelings of rejection."

Later in the meeting the group discussed "the possibility of going out for a Chinese meal. Christopher was rather pointedly not invited to this". The social worker summarized the mood of the meeting as "Lively and excited about the holiday, but there were undercurrents of feeling against Christopher which did not surface." ˙

Eventually Christopher's verbal aggression turned to physical aggression, first against someone in the hostel, and then, towards the end of March, in The Cherries itself. Here we quote at length from the diary.

"This was the last Sunday of Christopher's week at the group home. Christine and I were in Cathy's room when we heard the commotion and Roger (a new weekender) knocked on the door and asked us to come because Martin was bleeding. Christopher had hit him and they were all in Martin's room. Roger and Christopher were administering salt and water to him, and we got Cathy's Dettol. Martin was curled up on the bed crying. . . . It seemed that Martin hadn't hit back but that he had insulted him (i.e. Christopher) and this made him aggressive. Roger took Martin downstairs and made him some coffee, while Christine and I talked with Christopher. Christopher would not modify his behaviour and stated that he would do it again if anybody called him that. He seemed to be saying what you would expect from a boy that was brought up on . . . (a depressed housing estate in Slough). We countered this argument by saying that Roger was brought up on . . . and didn't act this way, but nothing could convince Christopher to change. Later I discussed the question with Ruth (Christopher's social worker, later to become one of the group home social workers) and rang the hostel, and we agreed that if he was not willing to change his ways he was not to go to the group home again."

At the group meeting the following day

"Christopher's behaviour was finally discussed. Christopher described his childhood and how he was beaten cruelly and referred to the environment on. . . . Then different environments were discussed, Barbara and Richard both talked about their background and we had a bit of group contagion with everybody going one better than the one before. Richard brought it back to reality, saying that the group home was different and that you have to control your aggression. By the end there seemed to be some sympathy for Christopher but we didn't discuss his coming again as the subject was hastily changed by Mary."

At the same time as this final confrontation with Christopher, the behaviour of Douglas was causing the group some anxiety. As mentioned before he became very unsettled when taken from the security of the hostel and although coping with the practicalities exhibited some disturbing behaviour e.g. swearing, sleeping all day, and not eating properly. Being a fairly passive person he caused little antagonism with the group, causing them to be anxious for his well-being rather than hostile. However, although the group seemed prepared to accept him, he was not able to make the final decision to move in. He finally decided to withdraw from consideration as a potential resident, a decision precipitated by his refusal to go on the group's holiday in early June.

Sally, however, seemed to be making steady progress during her weekend visits, despite problems with her epilepsy with entailed regular medication. Her friendly and cheerful disposition fitted in well with the group, and being about average in ability (among the residents) she

56

posed no problems of dependency. On the other hand, her abilities were not such that she constituted a threat to the established group hierarchy in the way that Christopher had done. In fact, coping with her epilepsy showed the capacity of the group not only to help one of its members, when in need, but also to deal with such an emergency situation without panic. The social workers later remarked that the group were far more capable than they at dealing with minor epileptic fits! Thus Sally's success reinforced the conclusion arrived at after the first year at the group home, that practical abilities are less important than personal factors in determining a person's chance of survival in the group situation.

The only other newcomer to The Cherries at this time was Roger.

*

ROGER

Year of birth 1945   I.Q. range 66–70

Parents – father: school caretaker, mother: domestic

Day special school up to the age of eleven, and then residential special school because of aggressive behaviour towards mother. After leaving school a series of short-lived jobs. Reported as having "a positive attitude to work but lacking confidence and over-sensitive". Complaints from neighbours and occasional aggressive outbursts led to brief hospitalization. Similar behaviour on discharge led to long term hospitalization from 1963. Thought suitable for discharge but due to very poor relationship with father and state of mother's health, alternative care was desirable. Therefore admitted to hostel 1973 prior to being considered for The Cherries.

Like Sally, Roger was a fairly quiet person, who, not unnaturally in his early days at the hostel, exhibited some signs of institutionalized behaviour. However, he had developed sufficiently by this time to warrant introduction to the group home via weekend visits. While at the hostel he had developed quite a strong relationship with Sally, but it was felt that since at this stage there was no certainty of them both being admitted to The Cherries, they should be kept apart during trial weekends, i.e. should visit at different times. The reason given for this enforced separation was to discourage a dependency on one another which would be pointless, if only one of them were to be admitted. It also provided the social workers with the opportunity to assess their individual capabilities. Roger, like Sally, fitted well into the group situation and after several weeks visiting the only major problem that remained was one of personal cleanliness. This was thought to be sufficient reason for further training prior to admission.

Thus, of the five aspirants early in the year, two, Douglas and Christopher, were by late May no longer under active consideration.

Sally and Roger, though still visiting on separate weekends were becoming members of the group, and Susan, having temporarily overcome her anxiety, returned to the picture just prior to the group's June holiday. Throughout her period of absence from weekend visiting Susan had kept in contact with the group, occasionally being invited by them for an evening. It was therefore a simple matter to bring her back into the group of potential residents.

While these more dramatic activities were occurring with the weekenders, the six residents were getting on with their lives quietly. They were, of course, involved with the various incidents described above, as they reacted with and to the newcomers, but other than this only three major events occurred prior to the change in social workers in the middle of the year. These will be considered shortly but, at the risk of repetition, some statement must be made about the 'normality' rather than the more unusual events.

What then, to try and answer the question most often put by visitors to The Cherries, was a typical day? The residents would rise at different times in the morning, depending on the time they have to be at work (including the training centre for those who attend) and the time it takes to get there. This usually allowed breakfast, for those who took it, to be prepared in reasonable comfort rather than the whole group crowding together into the single kitchen which serves the home. Breakfast over, they departed for work either by public transport or that provided by the Social Service Department e.g. training centre minibus. Returning from work in a similar random fashion enabled them to prepare their respective evening meals without hindrance. They did, on occasions, wait for everyone to be present if a 'special' meal was being organized. The rest of the evening would be taken up with various activities, determined, as with most people, by their particular mood at the time. Examples of these activities are watching television, visiting the local pub, going to the pictures, going out for a meal, and, for some, evening classes at the local technical college. This list is not exhaustive, but indicates the variety of activities undertaken by the group members either individually or as a group.

In addition, those in contact with their relatives had found that, once established as independent, they would visit their families with greater freedom from anxiety on both sides than had hitherto been the case. In summary, then, a lifestyle similar to that of a great number of 'normal' people was being enjoyed by a group whose members belong to a classification of people thought to be incapable of such living. This cannot be emphasized too strongly and should continually be borne in mind when considering the remainder of this book.

Returning to the three events mentioned earlier they will be described in the order in which they occurred. The first concerns the return of Martin and Doreen to the adult training centre after a period in open employment. Martin, showing some considerable initiative, took the risk of changing his job at a furniture warehouse for one with better pay working in the kitchens of a local hospital. This was not arranged for him and was at first welcomed since he had been the lowest paid of those in employment. Unfortunately Martin's cleanliness, unimportant in his previous job, was of an insufficient standard for the hospital and although warned about this, he was unable to adjust sufficiently to avoid being dismissed some weeks later. By this time his old job, a traditional first employment for trainees, had been given to Roger who had been attending the training centre. Unemployment at this time (i.e. March/April 1975) was still increasing and thus alternative work was not available and Martin returned to the training centre.

For Doreen, aggression rather than ambition caused her return to the ATC. After having controlled her temper for some time, Doreen went through a period of considerable depression starting in February 1975 and culminating in an outburst at work during which she hit a fellow worker and was dismissed. The diary describes this period. At a group meeting in mid-February "Doreen was very quiet and depressed throughout the meeting and finally I asked her what was wrong. She told us about her work and the problems there and everybody was sympathetic but this did not seem to cheer her up at all". In early March at a further meeting "there was a lot of anger because Doreen had been very moody recently". Although Doreen was found another job a few weeks later her depression had continued and a similar incident occurred. It was therefore decided that she should return to the training centre until her work behaviour stabilized and her depression decreased. It was not felt that this period would need to be very long, and in fact she did soon stabilize but, like Martin, found the employment situation impossible. She therefore remained at the training centre.

The other two events were of a much more positive nature, and in fact one has already been mentioned in passing. This was the holiday taken by the group in early June. An earlier chapter has described a camping weekend spent by the residents and social workers in the summer of 1974, and following discussion of various alternatives the group decided on a full week in self-catering chalets for this year. Although the holiday was booked and organized by the social workers, the residents participated far more in the planning and preparation for the week's activities than they had done for the camping weekend. They also undertook all the household tasks required by a self-catering holiday and received no special treatment from anyone in the chalet village. In fact it is doubtful whether they stood out from the rest of the holiday makers.

The 1975 holiday, although a 'different' event, is really only a further example of the progress of the group towards a 'normal' way of life. A more fundamental event however which has much wider implications than the simple survival of the group in the community was the marriage of Richard and Cathy on Saturday 14th June 1975.

The relationship between Cathy and Richard, as a result of which they were sharing a room, has been mentioned earlier, and this undoubtedly caused some controversy as it became more widely known. So too will their decision to get married and opinion will be divided, as before, among those who oppose any unsupervised mixing of sexes in residential accommodation for single people, those who think it all right for 'normal' people but not for the mentally handicapped, and those who maintain that mentally handicapped people have the same rights as other human beings. Beyond this moral argument, there are those who claim, at a more pragmatic level, that the mentally handicapped are incapable of understanding the responsibility involved in marriage.

On the first point, as one writer[52] notes, the United Nations Universal Declaration of the Rights of Mentally Retarded Persons, passed by the General Assembly in 1971 without a dissenting vote, contains these words in the first clause: "The mentally retarded person has, to the maximum degree of feasibility, the same rights as other human beings". Thus there is universal recognition at the highest level of international affairs of the rights of association between all mentally handicapped people. However, the same writer also points to the fact that "Britain lags far behind other civilised nations in their recognition of the full rights of the mentally handicapped," and blames a mixture of fear of public reaction and fear of the procreation of further handicapped people. George Lee, Secretary General of the National Society for Mentally Handicapped Children, argues this latter case as "the right of society at large to resist the unnecessary growth of the social, educational and welfare burdens arising from the birth of (such) a child"[53]. He concludes that "the mentally retarded should not be persuaded of their right to procreate." In the Britain of 1975 therefore most facilities for the mentally handicapped discouraged any form of sexual relations, both by exhortation, and by the sheer physical arrangements of accommodation.

We feel strongly that the rights of the mentally handicapped to as full a life as possible should be encouraged, and that this can only be achieved if sufficient attention is paid to the education of these people in all matters relating to a normal life, including relationships with the opposite sex. The education of the public at large to accept that the mentally handicapped possess these rights must also take place if this country is to fulfil its obligations under the United Nations Agreement. Only then will our level of service in this country reach that of the more enlightened countries in the world who, by taking the bold decision to allow these freedoms, have found, using Sweden as an example, that "tolerance and general satisfaction with life . . . increase, and that the retarded . . . become calmer and more interested in their appearance and behaviour"[54].

Even assuming the basic rights of association however, there are those who, as mentioned before, deny that the handicapped have the ability to undertake the responsibility of marriage. This is a more difficult area since it is undoubtedly true that some mentally handicapped people do not fully understand what is involved. However the same could be said of many 'normal' people, who enter marriage with little thought for the outcome. Thus, by denying the mentally handicapped the opportunity to make mistakes, even in something as serious as marriage, one is setting them apart from the rest of the population, when the experience of all who have tried it suggest that the most beneficial attitude is to encourage responsible behaviour. We repeat with added emphasis the definition of 'normalization' given in Chapter 2, "Normalization does not imply any denial of the retarded person's handicap. It involves rather exploiting his other mental and physical capacities so that his handicap becomes less pronounced. It means also that the retarded person has the *same rights and obligations* as other people so far as this is possible"[55].

Returning from the general to the particular, Richard and Cathy were considered to have gained a sufficient sense of responsibility to enable them to make such a decision. Both had very traditional views of marriage, Cathy seeing herself in the role of home-maker doing all the household tasks and generally 'looking after' Richard, while Richard adopted the masculine 'protective' role. The problem of children did not arise since, when this was discussed, they themselves decided not to have any. The best way to achieve this was for Richard to have a vasectomy and he agreed to do so. As Cathy said at the time "We don't want children because they might be spastic like me, not able to use their hands or arms properly, or they might inherit epilepsy from Richard".

After discussion with the social workers the anxious relatives soon realized that the couple were sufficiently mature to make the decision, and that they would both benefit from the step they were about to make. To quote Richard on the subject of his father "I think what really helped was when he came over for a meal which Cathy cooked. We talked and afterwards he said, 'You've picked the right one there.' "

During the months before the wedding Cathy and Richard were noticeably more distant towards the rest of the group than they had been previously. This was particularly so during social activities and by the holiday this was causing some resentment. However the imminence of the wedding delayed any serious ill-feeling, although Cathy and Richard did agree to try to join in more. Just before the wedding Richard said "We are worried the group might think we're going to back away from them because we've got each other, but both of us want to muck in as before." In fact they had the prime opportunity to do this since having just been on the group holiday they decided to wait some time before going away for their honeymoon and were thus living with the rest of the group as soon as they were married.

CHAPTER VII

A marriage, and other changes

"Change is not made without inconvenience, even from worse to better" Richard Hooker

From the end of May to early August, therefore, considerable changes took place in the group home. Not only were Cathy and Richard to be married, but the two social workers who had been involved with the group from the beginning were leaving within one month of each other. One was leaving to get married and the other was moving away from the area. They had, in any case, discussed the possibility of leaving the group home project since they felt that to be truly independent the residents should be able to accept other social workers, and not become too attached to particular individuals. Understandably this change provoked some reaction from the residents but it is indicative of the development of the group, and of course the skill of the social workers, that this did not last long or cause any permanent disruption.

One of the new social workers accompanied the group for the whole week of their holiday, with the other one going down for a visit, while the two existing social workers stayed with the group for half a week each. (The total number of 'residents' on holiday was in fact eight since the actual residents were accompanied by Sally and Susan). This was the early part of a gradual introduction of the two replacement social workers to the group. After the holiday, the wedding and its preparations took up a considerable proportion of the time, and for the rest of June one of the original social workers was still involved. It was thus not until the beginning of July that sole responsibility for the group home passed to the new social workers, but having had only about six weeks in which to try and form relationships with the group it was to be expected that these had yet to crystallize into firm friendships. In addition the style of social work evolved over the 18 months of the home's existence was inevitably related to the personalities of the outgoing people, and thus it took time for new personalities and styles of working to be accepted.

The new social workers summarized the reactions of the residents to the change over as follows:

"Mary was very dominant, challenging the new social workers to upset her, and frightened of their attitude. She seemed to be trying to find out whether they would be more like staff than friends. This changed abruptly when her mother died; she then became very dependent on Ruth (one of the two new social workers).

63

"Mary and Barbara made sly remarks about social workers but Barbara was openly very accepting. There was lots of testing out; whether social workers would come as friends 'out of hours'. We were often asked to coffee on Sundays.

"Doreen hardly ever spoke although friendly. She was unable to raise things at meetings but had temper tantrums at work (ATC). The social workers visited her at work for a few weeks and then Doreen calmed down, but she still doesn't raise things at meetings.

"Martin was quite accepting.

"Cathy and Richard always approached both social workers, never one or the other: they were frightened of offending. They had had quite a formal relationship with the previous social workers."

These reactions re-emphasize the various personalities of the residents and their various roles within the group. Mary as the leader, backed up by the brash Barbara, was the most active in 'trying out' the new social workers. Most of all, of course, the residents were anxious that the freedom that they had enjoyed should not be reduced by the change in social workers, and though the fears were most often expressed either directly or indirectly by Mary, they were felt by all the others.

The division between 'staff' and 'friends' is interesting here since it highlights the difference in the residents' minds between what they define as staff i.e. people who tell them what to do, and friends i.e. people who don't. They have placed the social workers in the latter category and hostel staff in the former. It is undoubtedly true, and earlier reference has been made to the fact, that a difference in attitude existed between these two groups of people. This fundamental disagreement had now gone beyond the initial anxieties of the 'unknown' Cherries environment alluded to above and may at this stage have owed more to the basic 'professional' divide which separates workers in residential care from those engaged in 'fieldwork'. This is not unique to the field of mental handicap, and has its roots in the organizational development of social service departments into their present form[56]. To the fundamental 'professional' disagreement is added dispute over the 'right' way to care for the mentally handicapped and more particularly the 'right' way for them to behave. There had undoubtedly been a tendency on the part of both pairs of social workers to allow the Cherries residents to make mistakes, whether these be of major or minor nature. On the other hand, staff of residential establishments, recognizing quite rightly the difficulties of getting mentally handicapped people accepted into the community, tend to the view that mistakes in socially acceptable behaviour by the handicapped are more serious than similar mistakes by others. In other words they feel that standards of social functioning must be that much higher than 'normal' if the handicapped are to be accepted into the community. Thus opinions on when a person is 'ready' for acceptance for community living, i.e. the group home in this case, will differ and had differed, resulting in some friction between the social workers and the hostel staff. There had also been a similar hostile reaction from some other residential care staff and training centre personnel in the county to The Cherries and its residents, and this returns again to the earlier argument about the rights of the handicapped to a 'normal' life. We have stated our view on this latter point, and feel that it applies here. The problem is a continuing one, and was to emerge again in The Cherries story.

Returning to the new social workers, two major problems arose during their first few months. The first has been alluded to in the summary of the change, and concerns the death of Mary's mother. In mid-August Mary's mother visited The Cherries in a drunken state and asked Mary for money. Mary refused and her mother left. The following day Mary's mother committed suicide. The traumatic effect of this on Mary was revealed at the group meeting a day later.

"Ruth arrived first and spoke to Mary in the hall (on the stairs crying). She was feeling guilty about her mother's death and anti social workers because she had been unable to contact them. Barbara was trying to comfort Mary. We calmed Mary by giving her Ruth's home telephone number and offered to cancel the group meeting but Mary insisted. In the discussion that followed we established that she was angry because she had been unable to contact social workers. We established that she was feeling guilty because her mother had come to The Cherries in the evening asking for money and was refused."

During the two weeks that followed Mary was very dependent on her contact with the social workers, and Ruth in particular. The social workers visited more often and Mary would ring up Ruth practically every day, often just to check that she was still there. By the time the funeral took place at the end of the month, Mary was becoming her old self again, although for some time afterwards she was very anxious to maintain contact with Ruth and know that she was available.

Ironically, of course, this tragedy had the effect of bringing the social workers closer to the group, and they were more able to diminish, if not resolve, the second major problem which had affected the group since the wedding of Cathy and Richard. The tendency to isolation of the couple prior to their marriage has already been noted and some ill feeling still remained.

After the marriage the problem was exacerbated in two further ways. First, Richard started to do less housework, seeing this as a wife's duty. Secondly there were considerable financial difficulties due to their changed circumstances. Both problems affected the group, the first in that it caused resentment from the other residents because Richard was not going his 'share', and the second in that Richard became very depressed over a sudden reduction in his income as a result of getting married. This latter change is illustrated by Table 2 below.

Cathy's finances actually improved on her marriage since she was able to claim the married person's tax allowance. This allowance would have

Table 2 Richard and Cathy's finances – before and after marriage

Circumstances		Gross weekly income	Tax and National Insurance	Disposable Income after rent
Not married	Cathy	£29.00	£7.21	£16.54
	Richard	19.10	—	13.85
	Joint	£48.10	£7.21	£30.39
Married	Cathy	£29.00	£1.60	£22.15
	Richard	4.95	—	0.30
	Joint	£33.95	£1.60	£21.85

been Richard's if he had been able to work, but since he attended a training centre the allowance, along with her own single person's allowance, went to Cathy. Thus her tax and National Insurance were considerably reduced.

Richard, who was dependent on supplementary benefit and his small wage of £2 from the training centre, suffered a considerable reduction in income. This was caused by the supplementary benefit rules which include the wife's income in the assessment of married couples. Richard's payments from the social security office were thus reduced from £17.10 to £2.95. Given that both partners were still paying the same rent as when single their combined disposable income after rent was reduced by just under nine pounds, and the amount of money which Richard could regard as his was reduced to virtually nothing. The problem was eased slightly in November 1975 by the introduction of Non-Contributory Invalidity Pension which is not means-tested, and which raised Richard's income to £9.90 per week. This, however, still left the couple some £3 worse off than before their marriage[57].

The social workers were able to alleviate, to some extent, Richard's depression at not being able to "support his wife" by explaining to him that Cathy's extra tax allowance had come about as a result of their marriage, and thus her extra income belonged to them both. The less pressing problem of the housework was fairly easily resolved by gradual pressure from the group backed by the social workers. The friction had therefore been eased by the normal process of group meetings and social work, but the desire of Richard and Cathy to have their own home remained. This raises the more general point of sub-groupings in the group home and although the particular division here was caused by a marriage, it is likely that once the numbers in a group reach eight or ten subgroups are bound to appear. Some of the reasons for The Cherries having accommodation for ten to twelve residents have been given earlier, and it is probably because of the original aims of bed-sitter type accommodation with staffing that sub-grouping problems were not foreseen. Were the local society now to be designing a group home i.e. a house for independent living for a group of mentally handicapped people, it is likely that no more than three or four people to any one unit of accommodation would be considered.

At this point, of course, the whole question of purpose-built accommodation could be raised, but the discussion will be deferred to the concluding chapters.

Certainly for Richard and Cathy the need, shared by most married couples, for their own accommodation was generally accepted. They were therefore placed on the council house waiting list in the hope that they would get a small bungalow. Later the idea of warden-supervised accommodation arose and this was seen as the most likely possibility. Their need for sheltered accommodation was seen to arise from their physical rather than their mental handicap and there was no implication that they were incapable of supporting themselves, but merely that a warden should be on call in case of emergency. Until this was available Richard and Cathy were encouraged to make the effort to participate fully in the life of The Cherries.

By participating in the solutions to the two problems of Mary's mother's death and the effect of Richard and Cathy's marriage, the new social workers had begun to establish relationships with the residents which would enable them to assist in the development of the group in the ensuing months. Soon after they had taken over responsibility it was decided that Sally and Roger, the most likely new residents, should undergo a further two months of social training, during which time they would not visit The Cherries for weekends. They were still invited by friends at The Cherries for social visits, but this period of training combined with the problems of the changeover had resulted in a decision not to arrange any weekend visiting in the short term. After the easing of the problems described above, weekend visits by all potential residents could be resumed and the pattern of Cherries life began to return to the settled ways of earlier in the year.

As the routine began to return towards the end of August the residents raised the question of weekenders and new members of the group. In particular, although they claimed to miss all weekenders, they wanted to know when Roger and Sally would move in. As already noted, Roger and Sally had paid social calls to The Cherries and this, combined with a longer visit over the bank holiday had increased the group's desire that they become residents. Matters were slightly complicated by a changing staff situation at the hostel, which had been without a full complement for some time, thus preventing Roger and Sally from receiving the intensive training prescribed for them. Although their practical abilities had undoubtedly improved, the hostel staff argued that they were not ready to move in. This caused some dispute between the social workers and hostel staff, exacerbated by the

67

'professional' differences mentioned earlier, since the social workers felt that the couple's social deficiencies were not sufficient to prevent the move, and that the delays had been an unfair burden on Roger and Sally. Eventually it was decided, at a more senior level, to allow Roger and Sally to move in, which they did in early September.

The arrival of Roger and Sally marked the beginning of a period of relative stability in terms of changes in residents in the group home. One major factor contributing to this particular stability was the relationship between the hostel and The Cherries. On the one hand staff shortages at the hostel, which had contributed to the delay in moving Roger and Sally, also meant that it was difficult to maintain a flow of weekend visitors. In addition, the hostel's anxieties over this couple led to a greater sense of the trial nature of their residence, thus inhibiting experimentation with any other new residents. Also, of course, with eight permanent residents in The Cherries, showing yet more signs of sub-grouping than had existed with six, it was becoming increasingly difficult to find people who would fit in happily with all of them.

In practice, then, the period from September 1975 until May 1976 showed little in the way of changes in The Cherries personnel, and was noticeable only in its minor problems and successes. The minor problems nearly all centred around the movement of Roger and Sally and the higher standards demanded of them by the hostel staff. The successes could be divided into two major categories; the development of the relationship with the social workers and within the group that led to more 'normal' living, and the increased public importance of The Cherries as an example of group home living for the mentally handicapped.

In greater detail, dealing initially with the minor problems, the first to cause significant anxiety was concerned with Sally's fits. As an epileptic Sally had already been on anticonvulsant drugs at the hostel. On moving to The Cherries it was thought that sufficient arrangements had been made, using the group competence to cope with the supply of these for Sally. As it turned out, it was not so much the supply as the particular sort of drugs which was to cause her and the group problems over the ensuing months. It is speculation to suggest that the move to The Cherries had affected Sally's make-up sufficiently to cause an increase in fits, but it is certain that by February her medication had been changed but her fits were still not fully stabilized. This problem was not great in itself, and by June we find the social worker reporting to the doctor on the decreased frequency of Sally's fits, but it served to reinforce the pessimistic view of the ability of Sally in particular, and the mentally handicapped in general to survive independent of residential supervision. This was made more explicit in the case of Roger, and the two newcomers still tended to be taken together in discussions about their suitability for The Cherries.

68

Roger's behaviour was more easily identified as unacceptable;

"Barbara said that Roger is lazy and does not either keep himself clean or do any washing and that he leaves all the cooking and washing up to Sally. Roger denied this emphatically." "Roger was not very clean and reputedly not doing any washing." "Complaints about Roger and Sally's washing left in the washing room and not taken back upstairs." "Still trouble with toilets not being cleaned, especially Robert and David."

Most of these complaints were brought up at group meetings over the four month period after Roger's arrival, but the situation was exacerbated following visits by members of the hostel staff to The Cherries where the same failings to maintain a good standard of cleanliness were observed and criticised. Despite the social worker's efforts to back up the comments of the group, which were achieving some positive results with Roger, the improvement had not been sufficient to satisfy anyone. However, some members of hostel staff felt that this was sufficient indication that Roger was unable to function satisfactorily in the group home, and so there was continued debate about his residence.

This again raised the general point of what is 'acceptable' behaviour for group home residents and who is to decide on the acceptability of it. The understandable desire on the part of dedicated hostel staff for conventional behaviour from their mentally handicapped residents may, as we have noted earlier, lead to a standard above that of many normal households being demanded. It can also result in a degree of intolerance of the initially lower standards which almost inevitably result from self supervision replacing staff supervision. The group, as we have seen, did not accept Roger's general lack of cleanliness, but were prepared, as were the social workers, to see him gradually improve, rather than have to reach their standards immediately. Everyone, however, was a little disappointed at his slow rate of progress. Since the social workers and the resident group were the major arbiters of 'acceptability' Roger remained at The Cherries but the differences of opinion did not improve relationships between the hostel and the group home.

By March this friction had reached sufficient pitch to be raised at a group meeting to which hostel staff were invited. It is a measure of how far the group had progressed that they were very agreeable to the matter being sorted out in this way and were able to state their views in front of the staff concerned. The group meeting seemed to clear the air and it is noted that "Arthur (the hostel representative) invited The Cherries group down to the hostel at any time. It was agreed that the hostel and The Cherries will have a joint social and group meeting. The group invited Arthur to come to meetings regularly."

As we have noted this reconciliation was in some part a feature of the group's stability. Beyond this, however, it also indicates the extent to which relationships between the two new social workers and the resident group had developed during the nine months since their arrival. This is one of the major successes of the stable period, and emphasizes still further the greater sense of independence and security felt by the residents. It also seems to us to point to the unsurprising fact that the more normally mentally handicapped people are treated the more normally will they respond. Further incidents confirm this view. It will be remembered that the puppy kept for a short period by the group had to be removed due to the group's lack of ability to look after it. Within a year, however, of the puppy's departure the group were sufficiently aware of the problems of keeping pets, and also sufficiently confident in what they wanted for their home, to have persuaded those responsible for The Cherries to allow them to keep another, older, dog. (By way of an aside the preponderance of pets that figure throughout The Cherries' history causes some speculation about the degree of social isolation experienced by mentally handicapped people and their delight in dealing with other living beings. Further anecdotal evidence from, for example, those involved with riding for the mentally handicapped suggests a fruitful line of investigation on the therapeutic effects of animals).

Other 'successes' of the period became almost mundane by their repetition. It is commonplace for people to go to pantomimes at Christmas, have New Year parties or go out to dinner to celebrate anniversaries. For the mentally handicapped to participate in such events is something of a surprise to many people. For them to initiate and participate in the organization of these activities would be more surprising still. Yet we find in the diary references to all these things taking place. For example "Mary said they had decided to go to the pictures and a Chinese meal in Slough" and "Cathy and Richard went for a meal on Cathy's birthday and all went to the Pied Horse for a drink on Sunday". Once again the other still more ordinary events of everyday living go unremarked, but their importance should not be forgotten. It should be remembered that by now the social workers were only visiting once or twice a week and yet they were not besieged with practical problems at every visit as had seemed to be the case earlier on. It is easy, speaking for the majority who have never been in any form of institutional care to think how routine it is to run a household. For those who have experienced lengthy periods of time when laundry was done, light bulbs and toilet rolls were replaced, and food prepared to a timetable, without their being involved in the decisions, the change to self management is quite dramatic. This should be continually borne in mind when considering the experiences of The Cherries' group. They were coping with their responsibilities, albeit with some support, but it is impossible, even in the space of a book to recount the hundred and one everyday activities performed by these so-called 'subnormal' individuals.

70

At this time, even after two years of existence, The Cherries was still fairly uncommon as a form of residential provision for mentally handicapped adults. This and the continued 'success' of its residents led to a large number of visitors, some of whom have already been mentioned. Two worthy of particular note were members of the current Committee of Enquiry into Mental Handicap Nursing and Care (The Jay Committee), and a film company in the process of making a documentary film about The Cherries.

The Jay Committee members visited The Cherries in February 1976. They were shown round by Barbara and then attended a group meeting, at which they discussed at great length holidays and daily living with the residents. Though possibly important nationally in terms of some effect on the committee's deliberations this visit did not have a great effect on The Cherries residents themselves. Of far more direct relevance to the group was the continued involvement throughout the latter half of 1975 of Platypus Films Ltd.

Having attempted somewhat unsuccessfully to video-tape activities at The Cherries for the purposes of this research, it was decided that a more useful permanent record could be established using professional film-makers. Additional funds were found for this purpose from Slough Mencap and the DHSS and we were fortunate in finding a company prepared to risk the rest of the cost from their own resources. The resultant film, premièred in June 1976, has unfortunately received no national showing, but through outlets to local societies and local authorities, it has widened awareness of The Cherries project and the possibilities of group home living. For the residents, who participated fully throughout the film, in their view the film was an accurate portrayal of life at The Cherries. Particularly pleased were Richard and Cathy who had the opportunity to see their wedding on film.

On the whole, then, the lack of changes in residents meant that the period was a quiet one for The Cherries project. As the next chapter will show, the quiet was not to last for long.

CHAPTER VIII

Steps forward and steps back

"If you can meet with Triumph and Disaster, and treat those two imposters just the same"
R. Kipling – *If*

By June of 1976 the stability of the previous nine months came under threat. This was due to circumstances, at first encouraged by supporting staff, which then got rather out of hand. These circumstances centred around Mary's family. As we have already seen, Mary, more than any of the other Cherries residents could justifiably be described as someone with a socially produced handicap rather than any organic problem. As part of a large family, known to the social services for a number of years, Mary fits all too well into the classic 'cycle of deprivation'. Like many children of such families her progress through various systems of local authority care was somewhat haphazard, and eventually she found herself with the label 'mental handicap'. On many criteria now used for judgement such as social competance or I.Q. she would not be so classified today, but having been in the system she has proved an immensly useful member of The Cherries group.

During the two years she had been at The Cherries she had maintained contact with her family, and, in fact, had used the support of The Cherries to come through the traumatic period of her mother's death. Whether this event released certain restrictions on the behaviour of her brothers and sisters is a matter for speculation but it is certainly true that the frequency of their contact with The Cherries seems to have increased during the first half of 1976. Mary was, by now, sufficiently confident in the independence of The Cherries in the residents' power over what took place there to start inviting members of her family for visits. At first the contact was encouraged, as being not only useful to Mary, but also as being a sign that The Cherries was becoming a home to which, like any other home, residents could invite whomsoever they wished. Encouragement continued in a more formal way when one of Mary's sisters, who lived nearby, was appointed as the official home help for The Cherries. Unfortunately, particularly because of the availability of bed space even with eight residents, Mary's hospitality was open to abuse, and abused it was.

At first it was just a question of one of her brothers or sisters staying for a night but then, first with one particular brother, and then with her sisters this developed into something approaching permanent residence. The brother, being still fairly young, did evince some sympathy from the social workers when he became homeless and thus was tolerated as a temporary lodger. He also had serious problems with his health, and it is another somewhat dramatic demonstration of the group's capabilities, that when his health deteriorated to the point of a heart attack, they coped calmly and adequately with the emergency. Mary's brother thus spent some time in hospital, after which alternative accommodation became available. Whilst it could, quite reasonably, have been argued that by putting up her brother in an emergency, Mary was giving normal and quite commendable support to her family, it is less easy to justify the use of The Cherries made by three of her sisters.

Having remained reasonably passive and accepting of Mary's relatives initially, the group did begin to express certain objections to some of the things they started to do. The first major problem concerned a married sister who had left her husband and come to The Cherries with her boyfriend to take up residence. This did not suit the group, but their objections did not carry much weight with the sister who tended to dominate Mary. Further, they were in the somewhat ambivalent position of there being the precedent of Mary's brother. At this point the social workers felt it necessary to intervene as Mary's generosity was clearly being exploited. In addition to the sheer fact of the couple's presence at The Cherries, there was problems with the girl's husband visiting and pestering, not only his wife, but Mary and the group as well. This was to continue after the social workers had managed to evict the couple, to the extent that a solicitor's letter was necessary to warn the husband about harassing The Cherries residents.

Over the ensuing months more problems arose with other members of Mary's family, with complaints about the efficiency of the sister acting as a home help and the use made by her and another sister of The Cherries as a place to bring their boyfriends. The problem dragged on throughout the summer of 1976 eventually creating a small amount of publicity in the local paper, which, combined with the continued efforts of the social workers, seemed to halt the abuses without destroying the family contact completely.

Part of this problem was, of course, caused by available bed space at The Cherries, and part by the peculiar nature of Mary's family, and thus the wider implications should not be over emphasized. It does, however, raise the general problem, when considering future group homes for the mentally handicapped, of how much freedom residents should have over their visitors. Like many other of the freedoms which the 'normal' person enjoys, the freedom to chose one's friends and one's degree of association with them is accepted. However we again come up against the genuine problem of the exploitability of the mentally handicapped and the responsibility for protection of the caring services. As elsewhere in this book, we would advocate the greatest possible availability of the normal freedoms of everyday life, and it seems to us that the social services in dealing with Mary's family successfully walked the narrow tight-rope between total freedom and undue repression very well.

In the middle of the summer, while these events were occurring, a new warden was appointed to the hostel. This had taken some time since the departure of the previous incumbent, and the delay had tended to inhibit consideration of new residents for The Cherries. Once the hostel began to have settled staff, however, further potential Cherries residents started to emerge, gradually over the period from June to September. One of these, Tina, will be remembered as a previous resident who had been returned to the hostel as a result of group pressure following her refusal to work and pay rent. The others were Cheryl and Bob.

*

CHERYL

Year of birth 1920   I.Q. range 56–60

Parents – father: occupation unknown, mother: deceased

Mother died when Cheryl was six. Father could not cope and so Cheryl was placed in a home. Her behaviour was violent and destructive which led to admission to Rampton hospital. Discharged from there to a mental subnormality hospital in 1962 and from there – via the hospital's hostel to the Slough Hostel in 1976.

*

BOB

Year of birth 1940   I.Q. range unknown

Parents – father: deceased, mother: occupation unknown

Bob is the fourth child in a family of five. His childhood appears to have been deprived. There were difficulties at school and he was described as lazy. He ran away from home on several occasions. On leaving school had difficulty in maintaining continuous employment. Was admitted to a mental handicap hospital for approximately one year, 1962–1963. His problems at home continued and he was referred to the Social Services Department by the Probation Service following a series of court appearances due to aggressive behaviour. In 1976 was admitted to hostel in Slough, from sleeping rough.

Cheryl arrived at the hostel from the local mental handicap hospital in July, having been reviewed at the hospital by the group home social workers who considered her to be a possible Cherries resident. Like all other people who moved from hospital to the group home, such as Doreen, Cheryl was given a reasonable period for settling into the hostel before starting weekend visits to The Cherries. Initial worries were not about her general competence but mainly centred on her standards of personal hygiene. Bob on the other hand had been at the hostel for some time. At a case conference at the beginning of September he was considered to be a suitable resident for The Cherries with the rider that his tendency to "relate strongly to staff as opposed to residents ... may cause problems with the group at The Cherries". Despite this reservation he was introduced as a weekender some three days later.

At the same time Tina was becoming a regular weekend visitor again. Given her previous experience with the residents, and the fact that she had been holding down a job for some time it is not surprising that following this brief period of weekend visiting a case conference in October decided that "she should move in but continue going to the hostel for lunch as this offers additional support. Philip (the hostel warden) would liaise with her employers".

Over the next few months Bob and Cheryl continued to be appraised by both the social workers and the residents. Cheryl's tendency to monopolize the attention of the social workers at every opportunity continued to be a problem, as did elements of her personal hygiene. Bob, whilst fitting in fairly well with the group, exhibited some of the usual behaviours of potential residents given the freedom of The Cherries. All this activity however, was overshadowed later in the year by Roger's problems.

In November the social workers were summoned to Slough Police Station to deal with Roger, who had been arrested after an incident with a teenage girl. We will not go into details of this here, but in order to obtain Roger's release on bail it was necessary to return him to the staffed supervision of the hostel. This incident coincided with the departure of one of the social workers to have a baby and her replacement by Linda, one of the original two social workers who had returned to the Social Services Department. At the beginning of December Linda visited Roger at the hostel to discuss the offence and its possible implications.

"He seemed to have settled in alright but was very distraught at the possibility that he might have to go back to the hospital. At this point we were reassuring saying that we would do everything we could to keep him in the hostel as the offence seemed a fairly minor one."

At this stage, as the above quotation indicates, there was not thought to be any serious problem, and matters were pursued with the various legal authorities. While these continued, developments in The Cherries story, exacerbated possibly by the shadow of Roger's problem, suffered a slight reverse with the return of tension between the hostel and the group home. As well as this tension, the imminent arrival of four council house places for Cherries residents, the subject of long negotiations by the social services department and others, increased anxieties and uncertainties.

Tension between the hostel and the group home has been mentioned several times before and various possible reasons suggested for its frequency. This latest episode seems no more than a further demonstration of the difficulties experienced by different professional groups with different understandings and different standards of behaviour for those under their care. A major row was sparked off in early January by an incident involving staff and residents from the hostel and The Cherries group. As the following lengthy extract from the diary indicated, not only this major incident, but a number of minor aggravations existed between the two groups. It should be remembered that the diary is written by the group home social workers and therefore we get a somewhat one sided view, but the sense of disagreement is clearly indicated.

"In the week between the last meeting and today's, there had been various phone calls to Ruth, and to Linda verbally when she took the group home dog to the vet on the Friday, complaining about Philip and the hostel. We had therefore ensured that Philip was present at the meeting.

"There was various discussion in a general way about jumble, and various other general chit-chat until we got down to the three main areas of aggravation between the hostel and the group home.

"We learned, that on Sunday morning, Joe (a member of the hostel staff) and a group of about 16 residents from the hostel had walked into the group home without announcing their arrival in advance, had walked through the kitchen ignoring the group home residents who were there and had gone up to the television room and asked for coffee. The group home group had been very angry that all these people should walk into their kitchen without knocking, without being invited and they seemed to have expressed this anger fairly freely. Mary had rung the hostel and complained about "the tribe of people that had walked in". There followed a quite heated discussion about the rights and wrongs of the whole communication between the two sides. On the one hand, Mary and the rest of the group were complaining because all these people had walked into their living room unannounced and Ruth and Linda supported them, feeling it was unreasonable for people to walk into one's living room and that we in our houses would not welcome such behaviour from friends however close, and would prefer a phone call first or for at least the people to knock before entering. Philip did not enter into any discussion of the rights and wrongs of turning up in people's living rooms unannounced and not talking to the people sitting there but complained about Mary's rudeness and inability to control her temper. Unfortunately, he insisted in phrasing his argument in a very pedantic and literal way, thus outwitting the residents who, being mentally handicapped, are not equipped to do verbal battle on a high intellectual level. They did their best to keep up with his argument and seemed to pick up the feeling that because he was staff he felt himself to be in the right. One of his main complaints was that Mary had referred to the group of visitors as a 'tribe'; this he seemed to find extremely abusive, although Mary tried to reassure him that it was not such a terrible thing to call them, referring to the fact that the previous warden and his wife would refer to them as a 'tribe' when they had been at the hostel. Philip seemed unconvinced of this. The net result was that no understanding was reached on either side as the group home group continued to remain aggrieved about the incident and Philip continued to remain aggrieved about their reaction to the incident. Nothing was resolved but Ruth and Linda stressed that visitors were expected to ring first to see whether it was alright to visit and that they themselves if they should happen to just drop in would always knock and ask if it was alright and never dream of just walking into the group home as if it was some kind of institution where the residents have no say in who came and when.

"The next problem to be aired was Martin's premium bond. Martin stated that Philip had received a postal order or something similar through the post which he had not allowed Martin to have and would not let anybody else take down to Martin. In fact it turned out there had been some lack of understanding on Martin's part. The actual facts of the matter were that Philip had been looking through the safe and right at the bottom had found a premium bond in Martin's name which obviously dated from the time when Martin had lived at the hostel. He had told Martin of its existence when he saw him at the training centre, saying on the Tuesday that he was unable to give it him at that moment because he did not have the keys on him and asking Martin to call in at lunch time for it. Martin had jumped to the wrong conclusion that it had just arrived in the post and when he had gone back at lunch time as arranged, Philip had had to go out so there had been no clarification of what was involved. Martin had still not managed to get his hands on the premium bond and arranged to go and collect it from Philip during the week. Mary explained that it was a premium bond that Martin had bought with some money that had been given to them when they were engaged and living at the hostel.

"The final bone of contention was a budgerigar that Tina had given to the hostel. She had mentioned to us on the occasion that we had interviewed all the residents separately about the Council house, that she had had two budgerigars that had started to fight and that she had had to separate them. She had told us then that she was concerned that the hostel were not looking after the budgerigar that she had given to them properly and that she had therefore said that Cathy could have it as Cathy was talking about getting a budgie ready for when they moved in to the Council house. Apparently, Cathy had rung the hostel and in a rather tactless way had announced to them that she was going to have the budgerigar that Tina had given them because it wasn't being looked after properly. The hostel had been very annoyed about this. Cathy had then said that Sally had said it was being neglected and then Sally had come to the phone and said that she had not said it and everybody was blaming everybody else for saying the bird was neglected and the hostel was getting very angry about the whole thing. When all this came out into the open, Cathy burst into tears, Richard stomped out of the room and everybody started denying that anybody had said that the bird was being neglected. Ruth and Linda were able to shed some light on the matter as Tina had actually said to them that she had thought that the bird was not being looked after properly. We ordered Cathy to stop crying and explained exactly what she had done and we went over the events and the phone call. Philip said that Derek was caring for the bird very lovingly, changing its sand paper every day and had been terribly upset by the suggestion that he was not looking after it properly. Ruth and Linda tried to pour oil on troubled waters saying to Cathy that now she was reassured that the bird was alright she could get herself one of her own and that Tina need not worry any more as we had reassurances from Philip that the bird was in good hands. Linda suggested that if Derek was so offended about what they had all been saying, perhaps the group should send him an apology. There was a long silence at this, broken only by Mary who said that she wasn't going to apologise because she had never said it in the first place and this is how the matter was left.

77

"All in all the meeting was very unproductive, with no rapprochment between the group home and the hostel and it is interesting to note that Philip did not attend any group meetings after this; in fact he left this group meeting by taxi and Roger had to ask Linda for a lift back to the hostel for himself."

The incidents in themselves are, of course, quite trivial, as were problems that had arisen in previous years with different staff and different residents. In many ways the hostel staff were in a very difficult position, seen as dictators by those of The Cherries group resentful of their lives being organized, and the somewhat authoritarian invasion of staff and sixteen residents was almost bound to cause friction. In addition some of the basic, routine discipline considered necessary for some of the more handicapped individuals at the hostel was viewed with hostility by the more independent Cherries group, who had developed their own code of self-discipline. Staff in residential care must, by the very nature of their job, get used to making decisions about the lives of those in their care, almost always with the best of motives. A venture such as The Cherries which denies the very need for residential care staff must represent a threat not only to their raison d'être, but also to the basic ground rules under which they operate. It seems that despite staff changes at the hostel the same basic attitudes remained towards The Cherries as those highlighted in its earliest days.

It might have been thought that three years of co-operation would have led to a decrease in friction, but the incidents described above show that The Cherries residents still displayed sufficient insecurity in outlook towards the hostel to seize upon trivial incidents. The hostel staff in their turn, still saw such immature views as justification for them to take a dominant position, and thus communication between the two groups returned to a low point.

This did not present an optimistic prospect for those in charge of the group home since as mentioned above, active consideration was being given, not only for some separate form of accommodation for Cathy and Richard, but also to the group of four people likely to move on from The Cherries to a Council house. Whoever moved on, only two or three residents would be left in The Cherries and so active co-operation with the hostel was vital if it were to continue to be fully utilized.

The idea of a Council house for a group of The Cherries residents had been raised very early on when it was quickly seen that The Cherries building itself could never represent a 'normal' home. Lengthy negotiations had taken place with the local Housing Department with a view to obtaining one of the properties on the estate under construction in the immediate vicinity of The Cherries. Despite establishing the basic agreement to such an idea, these negotiations had been fraught with problems, largely due to the very novelty of the group home concept. Although Slough Social Services Department had evidence of similar council house utilization within the same county, dispute as to whether the full 'economic' (non-subsidized) rent was to be charged occupied most of 1976. It is still unclear why groups of people, as opposed to families, living in council housing have to pay the full non-subsidized rent when experience elsewhere indicates a number of groups operating under normal, subsidized, conditions. Problems over finance were the major cause of delays in the provision of an actual house, although other minor complications arose from time to time.

By the end of 1976 however, it was clear that a house was going to be available fairly shortly and the problem arose of the selection of the four people to fill it. Obviously Richard and Cathy were not in contention since they were on the normal waiting list for their own sheltered accommodation. The weekend visitors Bob and Cheryl also clearly did not qualify for consideration, nor, because of his current problem did Roger. This left four to be chosen from six, Barbara, Doreen, Martin, Mary, Sally and Tina. After lengthy deliberations four were selected and it was decided to tell them as quickly as possible in order that preparations could be made. The problem of course concerned the two who were not to make the move.

"Ruth, Linda and Neil (the Assistant Divisional Director) met at The Cherries in order to tell the group who was going to move into the Council house as the anxiety provoked by their not knowing was beginning to cause a lot of unsettled feelings. The main problem was Barbara who was all packed ready to go to the Council house and was absolutely impervious to all hints and suggestions that she might not be going and short of actually telling her point blank that she was not, we failed to convey to her that she was staying at the group home. The rest of the group were saying that they would not move to the Council house if Barbara went with them, because she still came back drunk occasionally, was very loud and aggressive and would generally get them a bad name with the neighbours".

We saw everybody separately as follows:

"*1. Barbara:* Neil spent a long time explaining to Barbara that we could not always have what we wanted and that it was not always pleasant having to tell people things because you sometimes had to tell them things that were not what they were expecting to hear. Barbara still did not catch on to what was coming and finally we had to spell out to her that she was going to stay at the group home and not move to the Council house. She was very upset, protesting that she was a model citizen, but we explained exactly why she wasn't going and told her that she would have to work on her problems in the hopes of going later or to another Council house should we be given one. She was very put out by this and not at all in a good mood about the whole thing.
"*2. Tina:* she had only recently moved to the group home and had said that she did not want to go to the Council house. We still saw her anyway, as we wanted to take the opportunity of seeing everybody individually and in particular we needed to have a go at Tina about her bad work record recently. We were all very cross with Tina because she had not been going to work, threatened her with not staying on at the group home and said that we would review the situation at the end of the month.

79

"*3. Mary:* when we interviewed Mary, she sat there thumb sucking and rocking until we told her that she was actually going to the Council house. We then stressed that they would have to keep the place nice, not make too much noise and be very considerate to the neighbours.

We also saw Sally, Martin and Doreen, who were also chosen to go to the Council house and stressed all these things to them too. We told Sally that Roger would not be able to go to the Council house now and we felt it might cheer her up to be allowed to go on her own. We told Martin that he would have to tidy up or else, as his standards left too much to be desired.

"Later on Barbara and Tina were found both sobbing in Mary's bedroom and Linda and Ruth had to comfort them both. The fact that they were both in our bad books had brought them close together and for the next few days they were seen together and seemed to have formed an alliance. They were very clingy and we had to try and console them by saying that somebody would have to stay behind and help Linda at the group home or she would not have anyone to go down and visit".

Barbara's 'problems', alluded to in the above diary extract, have, of course, been noted throughout The Cherries narrative, and it is interesting that even the social workers, who seemed willing to tolerate her behaviour more than most, still drew the line at this last crucial stage. Probably, like, ironically, the hostel staff with whom they had often disagreed, those responsible for The Cherries felt the need for an 'acceptable' group to go into the Council house. Of those in contention the competent, and reasonably well behaved Mary and Doreen were obvious candidates, and they could control, in many senses of the word, the other two, Martin and Sally. Poor Barbara, because of the frequency of her visits to pubs, and the occasional bout of rowdyism as a result, had ruled herself out. As well as being of concern to the social workers though, there are several references throughout the diary to the concern shown by the group over the bad name they felt that Barbara's drinking would give them.

Further preparations for the move continued into the new year of 1977, but they were somewhat overshadowed by further developments in Roger's case. This not only presents the last detailed part of The Cherries story but also shows the disparity of views that can be found of the subject of mental state even amongst acknowledged experts. Prior to Roger's appearance at the magistrates court

"Linda took Roger to A hospital (the nearest mental subnormality hospital) to see Dr. M. At this stage we were under the impression that Roger had made a feeble attempt to molest a teenage girl, had urinated on her, and that basically he did not really know what he was doing and the events had been more frightening than dangerous for the young girl. Dr. M felt that there was little point in raking up details of what had gone on, that Roger was not really a menace to society but that a mild tranquilliser, e.g. Valium, would help to keep him calm. It was agreed that he would write to the GP suggesting this and that we would arrange a follow up appointment in three months' time, by which time the court case should have been safely out of the way."

This reinforced the general feeling of sympathy for Roger felt by the social workers and expressed at a group meeting at about the same time.

"We also talked about Roger's offence; we had heard that Mary told Sally she should not have anything to do with Roger but none of this emerged at the group meeting where in fact the group gave every impression of wanting to continue its relationship with Roger and concern was expressed as to whether Philip would allow him to go down there for their Disco. Ruth and Linda promised to check on this."

A shock was in store, however, when in the first week of January

"Linda took Roger to Slough Magistrates Court where we were anticipating that his case would be dealt with. However, much to everybody's surprise, including the solicitors, the prosecution asked for it to be committed to Crown court in Reading presumably because they were hoping for a stiffer sentence than the magistrates could pass. The solicitor also got his hands on all the statements that had been in the police possession and all this seemed to make the offence much more serious than we had previously imagined. We then had to go through all the palaver of bailing Roger again, which involved getting Philip down from the hostel to sign the papers. Roger then returned to the hostel."

Following this setback, it was decided that Roger should undergo further psychiatric examination prior to the Crown court appearance. The contrast in opinion seems to us somewhat striking. Two weeks later

"Linda took Roger to see Dr. N at B Hospital (the nearest psychiatric hospital). This appointment had been arranged by the solicitor in the hopes of getting Dr. N to testify in court that Roger was alright to come back to the hostel and to avoid him being institutionalized because after the new evidence that had come to light and the witnesses' statements that we had not seen before, it looked much more serious than we had all originally thought. It now turned out that Roger had not merely urinated over the girl, because the samples of clothing sent to the laboratory proved to have semen stains on them. Dr. N gave Roger a lengthy interview, coupled with a physical examination in which he concluded that Roger was capable of intercourse but would experience pain in attempting it and said that he felt he was a menace to society and while safe during his period on bail, might well attempt the same thing again at some point in the future.

"Roger was very shaken after his interview with Dr. N and Dr. N said that he felt he was very depressed and should have a careful eye kept on him in case he should deteriorate and need sectioning and recommended that he be given some extra valium tablets to calm him down and keep him going over the weekend."

"Roger was all set to go straight down to the group home after his appointment at B hospital but Linda suggested that he should go back to the hostel, feeling after what Dr. N had said that Philip should have a look at him as he is in his care and that it would be a good idea for him to be given extra valium. On arrival at the hostel, Philip stated that he did not feel Roger was depressed and refused to give him any more valium than the GP had prescribed stating that he could not tamper with drugs and could only prescribe the amount the GP had stated. However it turned out that nobody had given Roger his valium for that morning as Philip had not been up, and he was able therefore to take that and he was given the necessary money and tablets for the rest of the day at The Cherries. While he was at the hostel, Sally rang to see how Roger was and sounded very supportive and warm and with Philip's blessing, Roger then went down to spend the rest of the day at the group home."

After another two weeks

"Linda took Roger to C hospital (the hospital from which Roger had initially been transferred to the hostel) for an interview with Dr. P. Without mentioning it to anybody, Dr. N had written to Dr. P asking him to admit Roger. We were able to explain the situation fully, Dr. P felt that it would be a shame to re-admit Roger but that we should have a Section 60 lined up for the court as otherwise they might send him to prison if they felt unable to let him return to the community. He undertook to write to Dr. M and arrange who would offer the bed."

Still further confusion was raised when

"Linda took Roger to see the solicitor. He went through all the statements with Roger and it came out that Roger had absolutely no grasp of sexual vocabulary, does not seem to know what he is doing or what he is supposed to do and needs the basic facts of life explaining to him. He also tries to cover up all the time because he thinks people will think he is stupid if he shows his ignorance, therefore quite likely to admit to all sorts of terrible perversions simply because he will not say that he does not know what they are. We agreed that once the court case is safely over, someone would undertake to explain things to him but that telling him now would only confuse matters more."

When the case finally came to the Crown court, Ruth took Roger to Reading where despite pleas that Roger should be returned to the hostel the court decided that this would not be suitable. Thus Roger returned to hospital C on an order under section 60 of the Mental Health Act. He was very distressed by the whole affair, but because of the way the social workers had been preparing him for this eventuality he settled down very well there.

The Cherries story did not, of course, stop when our research project came to an end, but we have now reached the point in the narrative where our involvement with the group home ended. Before going on to discuss the implications of the project we would like to complete the factual details of The Cherries group up to the time of writing (April 1978).

Just after Easter of 1977, Mary, Sally, Doreen and Martin moved into the Council house. Doreen has since moved back to The Cherries, being replaced in the Council house by Bob. A week after the Council house group had moved, Richard and Cathy themselves moved into a shel-tered flat. They have remained there ever since. The Cherries now contains five residents, Doreen, Tina and Barbara having been joined by Cheryl, the last weekend visitor mentioned in the narrative, and Derek, one of the original six potential residents from the very start of the project. A further resident new to the area is shortly to move in.

Roger remains in hospital, though there is hope of his returning to the hostel in the near future.

CHAPTER IX

Conclusions on The Cherries

"Something between a large bathing machine and a very small second class carriage" W. G. Gilbert—*Iolanthe*

In trying to assess the implications of The Cherries experiment we will consider two distinct aspects. The first is specific to The Cherries itself and is concerned with how far the project has achieved its stated aims and objectives. The second looks at The Cherries as a group home, and discusses the place of group homes in the overall system of provision for mentally handicapped adults. Each will be considered in turn in these last two chapters.

Starting with The Cherries itself then, it should at once be stated that, had the building not been provided by Slough Mencap, a group home for mentally handicapped adults would not have existed in Slough at the end of 1973. If, therefore, a number of the following comments appear to be critical of The Cherries project, the fact should be borne in mind that without Mencap's efforts there would have been no project to criticize.

As a general statement, we feel confident in saying that the benefits of the project, both in terms of individual benefits to specific people, and of lessons learnt about independent living for the mentally handicapped, have made the investment of time and money well worthwhile. To go into more detail, however, it is necessary to return to the aims and objectives of The Cherries experiment, outlined in Chapter II. These fell under the headings of:

i. Group Home as Home
ii. Origin and characteristics of residents
iii. Support services
iv. Finance.

Chapter II went on to give details, first of the major objective:

1. *Group Home as Home*

"The main objective is to provide a place of residence for twelve mentally handicapped persons. The intention is that the residents should regard it as home, and no pressure should be put on them to move on to more independent accommodation, although if they express a wish to do so, help in this should be given. The group home is not intended for persons already able to live in a less protected situation or in independent accommodation."

Clearly The Cherries has yet to provide a place of residence for *twelve* mentally handicapped persons, and it is doubtful whether, given its

84

current design and usage, it ever will. In fact, it appears to us that many of the problems arising in The Cherries project have come about as a result of the quantitative element of the first basic objective. Attempting to provide for twelve individuals in one single unit has not only militated against the intention to provide a 'home' for the residents, but, by the continuing available space and the pressure to fill the home, has brought about a number of the incidents described in the narrative. In more detail, the problems brought about by the basic design of The Cherries can be divided into two main areas. First the fundamental, physical, failings of the building itself, and second, problems arising within The Cherries project from the fact of having a twelve-bedded house with which to deal.

On the physical side, some of the faults perceived by the residents could be described as matters of taste and thus another group might not have expressed as much of a desire to change the decoration or the layout of rooms as did The Cherries residents. More fundamental, however, in terms of the design, is the concentration of basic service facilities, particularly the kitchen, for use by twelve people into an area not much bigger than that provided for such facilities in an average house. The residents themselves criticized the idea of having a kitchen/diner, and sought some sort of partitioning, and it seems to us that by trying to build facilities for twelve, whilst retaining a 'domestic' atmosphere, a compromise was reached which was far from satisfactory. Thus, for example, the need for shared rooms, the use of industrial-type carpets necessitating industrial-type cleaners, and the change to continental quilts which were unfamiliar to new residents all smack of an uneasy alliance between ordinary living and institutional economies. Even without ever having a 'full house', these problems have been obvious to staff and residents, and it all seems to relate back to the basic difficulty of building an 'ordinary' home for twelve people when there are practically no 'ordinary' homes built for that number.

Possibly more serious than the physical anomalies found in The Cherries are the problems caused to the developing group, and therefore to the project, by the fact of its being designed for twelve people. The largest and most basic of these problems is the extreme difficulty of trying to get that number of people to live together in harmony. We have mentioned earlier how, at the beginning of the experiment, criteria for selection of residents was largely based on practical capabilities and did not really have regard to personalities. This contributed quite a lot to the breakdown of the early group of six and, as the project progressed, it became clear that obtaining a personality mix was more important than the particular abilities of individuals. The problems of trying to mix a small group of individuals, mentally handicapped or otherwise, together satisfactorily can be imagined. The task facing the Social Services in trying to set up a group of twelve is therefore seen in its true perspective. Inevitably sub-grouping was bound to occur, and occur it did, initially in the form of Richard and Cathy's separation from the other residents. Also inevitably, leadership clashes will arise, as they did between Mary and anyone else who threatened her supremacy. Thus Christopher, who might well have been an acceptable resident in another group, was forced out of The Cherries.

It is clear that no hard and fast criteria are at present in existence to determine who can, and who cannot form a satisfactory group, be it of size two or twenty. We would stress strongly the lack of predictability of success in the group situation of such traditional measures as I.Q. or social competance since, by concentrating on individuals, they do not make allowances for the shared skills of the group. What should be emphasized is the importance of a successful mix of personalities, although how this is to be measured remains a major difficulty, since no such methods have to our knowledge been discovered for any group of individuals. In The Cherries experience we see evidence of a group selecting its own members on the basis of how well they fit in with that group. Such selection amounts to the application of intangible criteria which must be unique to each group, and cannot be generalized in any meaningful way. After all who can define the processes by which 'normal' adults choose their own living companions? They do, however, have the 'normal' right so to choose, and applying the normalization principle in this case, therefore, those setting up group homes would do well to consider the views of potential residents about their preferred companions.

The basic problem of trying to find twelve people to live together in The Cherries had a number of other ramifications. These were largely due to the extreme difficulty of such a task, resulting in The Cherries being half empty for most of the time and in the need for a continuous flow of residents from the hostel. Understandably, because of their involvement with the scheme, there was pressure from Slough Mencap to fill The Cherries. Pressure was also, of course, forthcoming from within the Social Services Department, since a half used resource is not popular with councillors. Thus there was no time when it was possible to reduce the ties with the hostel. This, as we have seen, caused a number of conflicts of authority, particularly on who was 'suitable' for The Cherries, but also because of an implied authority maintained by hostel staff over The Cherries residents coming into conflict with the authority of the group home social workers.

The clearest condemnation of The Cherries as a home comes from the residents themselves, however, in their desire, expressed very early in the project, for council house accommodation, and in the fact that the group who moved on have proved rather more trouble free since that time. With the benefit of hindsight it is clear that no real 'home' can exist in a twelve-bedded house.

Having criticized the physical design of the house, and indicated how, we feel, this has reduced the effectiveness of The Cherries as a 'home', a number of positive points should be made on the success of The Cherries in the development of its residents. Again it is worth remembering the alternative had The Cherries not been built, and it leads one to wonder how many of the twelve mentally handicapped people now living in Slough, free from residential supervision, would be doing so without The Cherries.

We have dealt at length, throughout the narrative, on the greater maturity shown by residents after a period in The Cherries. This, we feel, is almost entirely due to the fact that The Cherries is an independent group home. The greater need for responsibility which independent living generates, combined, of course, with effective counselling by the social workers, has undoubtedly given the residents a greater ability to survive in the community. The making of mistakes, and learning from them, has benefited The Cherries people enormously, and in ways which a hostel regime, however liberal, could not allow to happen. Above all, the sense of determination of their own lives has, we think, proved the greatest result of The Cherries experience.

The major benefits of The Cherries therefore come from its being an independent group home. As indicated earlier this will be considered further in the final chapter, when the place of group homes is discussed. Returning to the basic objectives of the project however, our findings on The Cherries specifically are that the objectives of The Cherries being a 'home' has not been achieved, though a far greater sense of the need for a 'home' in The Cherries residents has been gained, together with valuable maturity and ability to cope with such a home. The reasons, we think, why the basic objective has not been met stem from the attempt to design a single living unit for twelve individuals and the impossibility of such a design being practical.

Consideration of the subsidiary objectives of The Cherries project shows a greater level of achievement:

2. *Origin and Characteristics of Residents*
    "a. the selection of residents is to be initially and principally from the Slough Mencap and within 'New Berkshire' but rather than keep places vacant, the search for residents may be extended to the rest of Berkshire
    b. residents are to be of either sex
    c. residents should be at work either in open employment or at one of the Adult Training Centres
    d. the age of the residents to be generally young rather than old, but a diversity of ages within the group is desirable
    e. there is to be a wide distribution of I.Q. within the group but with efforts made to encourage those with I.Q.s below 50 to become residents."

Success in achieving these objectives can best be seen from Tables 3 and 4 which give basic details on the fifteen people who were either residents or weekenders during the main period of our study (roughly December 1973–December 1976).

As the table 3 shows, nearly all the objectives were met in that:
a. all fifteen were from the Slough Mencap area
b. a mixture of the sexes was achieved.
c. all fifteen were either in open employment or at the Adult Training Centre
d. most of the residents were under 35, but the total range was between 20 and 46
e. a wide distribution of I.Q.s existed in the group, with a number under 50.

Whilst the achievement does give grounds for optimism in that a much wider range of people than had been thought possible are seen to be capable of independent living, the very general nature of these criteria mean that it is not possible to indicate from them, who, precisely, is likely to succeed in a group home and who not. Once again we repeat the conclusion that personality factors within the group seems to be the main criterion for success, rather than practical abilities or the more basic measures of age, sex or I.Q. A much more detailed study of a number of group homes would seem to be necessary to try and identify more exactly who is likely to survive in such settings.

The third objective is met with equal ease:

3. *Support Service*
"The group home is to be independent of residential support, but if necessary, to be given domiciliary help by social workers and home helps."

Clearly, as the narrative shows, The Cherries has been independent of residential support in the sense of permanent resident staff. Thus the main objective has been satisfied. The degree of social work support has been very varied in terms of quantity, though not, we are happy to say, in terms of quality. The variation in the level of support has come about in the following ways. First, a gradual reduction of visiting seems to have taken place whenever a stable group has been in residence with few, if any, newcomers for a few months. Second, by contrast, an increase in support has proved necessary when changes are occurring. This was particularly true when the social workers themselves changed, but also when a lot of newcomers were introduced or traumatic events such as the death of Mary's mother took place. In terms of lessons from the project, the point about the size of The Cherries returns, in that a number of the changes which brought increased social work activity were caused by movements, in and out, of residents. It is likely we feel,

Table 3   Summary of origin and characteristics of residents and weekenders up to December 1976

Name	Age at 31.12.76	Sex	IQ range and source	Connections with Slough area	Place of residence on first consideration as potential Cherries resident	Employment for period of project
Cathy	38	F	46–50*	Slough resident for over 3 years	Slough hostel	Factory worker
Susan	26	F	46–50 WAIS 1973	Hostel resident for over 3 years	Slough hostel	A.T.C.
Martin	27	M	41–45*	Hostel resident for over 3 years	Slough hostel	Furniture shifter/hospital worker to March 1975, A.T.C. thereafter
Derek	46	M	41–45 N/K	Slough resident since birth	Slough hostel	Open employment
Mary	27	F	81–85*	Hostel resident for over 3 years	Digs in Slough	Laundry worker
Tina	24	F	81–85 Stanford Binet 1960	Hostel resident for over 3 years	Slough hostel	Alternating periods of factory work and work at A.T.C.
Barbara	34	F	51–55*	Slough parental address	Hospital A	Factory worker
Douglas	32	M	81–85 WISC 1973	Slough parental address	Slough hostel	A.T.C.
Richard	34	M	66–70*	Hostel resident for over 3 years	Slough hostel	A.T.C.
Doreen	40	F	55–60*	Hostel resident for over 3 years	Slough hostel	Factory worker to April 1975, A.T.C. thereafter
Christopher	22	M	N/K	Slough resident for over 3 years	Slough hostel	A.T.C.
Sally	20	F	61–65*	Slough resident for over 3 years	Slough hostel	A.T.C.

89

Table 3—*continued*

Name	Age at 31.12.76	Sex	IQ range and source	Connections with Slough area	Place of residence on first consideration as potential Cherries resident	Employment for period of project
Roger	31	M	66–70*	Slough parental address	Slough hostel	A.T.C. to February 1975, furniture shifter thereafter
Bob	36	M	N/K	Slough resident for two years	Slough hostel	A.T.C.
Cheryl	56	F	56–60 Wais.	Slough parental address	Hospital A	A.T.C.

* Details of IQ tests and dates for these people given in Appendix I.

Table 4 Periods of training and residence of potential group home members

Name	Aug 73	Sep	Oct	Nov	Dec	Jan 74	Feb	Mar	Apr	May	Jun	Jul	Aug	Sep	Oct	Nov	Dec	Jan 75	Feb	Mar	Apr	May	Jun	Jul	Aug	Sep	Oct	Nov	Dec	Jan 76	Feb	Mar	Apr	May	Jun	Jul	Aug	Sep	Oct	Nov	Dec
Cathy	x	x	x	x	—	—																																			
Susan	x	x	x	- -	- -	x	x	x	x	x	x	x	x	x	x	x	x	x	x	x	x	x	x	x	x	—	—	—	—	- -	- -	- -	- -	- -	- -	- -	- -	- -	- -	- -	- -
Martin								—	—	—	—	—	—	—	—	—	—	—	—	—																					
Derek	x	x	x	x	- -	x	x	- -	- -	x	x	- -	x	- -	- -	- -	- -	- -	- -	- -	- -	- -	- -	- -	- -	- -	- -	- -	- -	- -	- -	- -	- -	- -	- -	- -	- -	- -	- -	- -	- -
Mary									x	x	x	—	—																												
Tina					x	x	x	—	—	—	—	—	—	—	—	—	—	—	—	—	—	—	- -	- -	- -	- -	- -	- -	- -	- -	- -	- -	- -	- -	- -	- -	x	x	x	- -	- -
Barbara					x	x	x	x		x	x	—	—																												
Douglas					x	x	x	x	x	x	x	x	x	x	x	x	x	x	x	x	x	—	—																		
Richard									x	x	x	x	x	x	x	—	—																								
Doreen													x	x	x	x	—																								
Christopher																		x	x	x	x	x	—																		
Sally																x	x	x	x	x	x	x	x	x	x	x	—														
Roger																			x	x	x	x	x	x	x	x	—														
Bob																																						x	x	x	x
Cheryl																																						x	x	x	x

Key ——— residence   x x x x training   - - - - - long term prospect that intense social work effort such as that found at the beginning of The Cherries project will accompany the opening of any group home, but that this should reduce rather more quickly than was the case with The Cherries, if future group homes are provided in ordinary houses. This point probably also applies to the need for home helps which, as we have seen, also varied at The Cherries in terms of quantity. At no time, however, did it extend to the point where the home help was doing all the housework.

The final objective of The Cherries project concerned finance:

4. *Finance*

"The overall cost per resident was assumed to be lower than in alternative staffed accommodation, and an objective is to see how far this assumption was justified. The residents are to pay the County Council an economic rent, supported, if necessary, by a Supplementary Allowance."

Like statistics, costs have been used to justify a number of conflicting points of view by simply presenting a different set of figures. In our "Progress Reports"[58,59] of The Cherries project we chose to use the average weekly revenue costs of various caring environments to try and examine how far The Cherries met the above objective. This has been criticized on the grounds that:

a. average costs hide the differences in staff time and resources used by different individuals within a given environment
b. by excluding capital costs (i.e. the costs of buildings) an unfair comparison is made between old units, whose capital has been paid off, and new ones, which incur large capital and interest payments.

Since we intend to continue using direct revenue costs for comparison, some answer to these criticisms must be made. On the first point, our answer is twofold. First, it is excessively difficult to measure exactly how much of the total staff and other resources each individual in, say, a hostel uses up. Even if you could do this for the variable resources of a hostel, such as staff time, how do you then allocate each individual a share of the overheads of the establishment? Even in the business world such allocation is a matter for accounting convention, which varies from business to business. Second, if the average for one establishment hides 'cheaper' individuals then by definition, it must also hide 'more expensive' individuals. If we assume, in the absence of other evidence, that the 'cheap' and the 'expensive' are distributed evenly about the average a fair comparison can be made using that average.

On the question of capital costs, the justification for excluding them seems rather more straightforward. If one is attempting to compare the costs of two different forms of care, then the major comparison should be how much each costs to run, i.e. the revenue costs. If capital costs, particularly in today's circumstances, were to be included, they would so mask this basic comparison as to make it almost meaningless. By all means, if new buildings are being considered, compare alternatives in capital terms, but we feel it is unfair to consider an old building, which is cheap in capital terms, as a representative of a particular type of care with a new, expensive one as a representative of another type of care. There is an unfortunate tendency to do this in mental handicap provision when, as we have argued, the need for purpose built accommodation is far less than is thought.

Given that we are concentrating on direct revenue costs therefore, how does The Cherries compare with other environments? Table 5 below shows the 1974/75 revenue costs for various combinations of living and working environments in Berkshire. Full details of how these figures are obtained are given in Appendix II, but, in outline, they consist of three main elements, i.e. cost of residential care, cost of day care and cost to the state in Supplementary Benefits or other Social Security payments. It should be noted that our revenue costs for The Cherries are based on an average occupancy level of six, rather than the figure of ten used in earlier reports. This is because of our expectation, for reasons given earlier, that The Cherries will never be completely full.

Table 5   Costs of various caring environments in Berkshire (1974–1975 costs)

Environment	Cost per person per week £
Hospital	51.34
Hostel/A.T.C.	40.17
Hostel/open employment	20.30
Home/A.T.C	18.97
Home/open employment	Nil
Group home/A.T.C. (Social Worker (SW) and Home Help (HH) costs included)	39.19
Group home/open employment (SW and HH included)	16.47
Group home/A.T.C. (SW and HH excluded)	29.01
Group home/open employment (SW and HH excluded)	5.29

Even in an under-occupied state, it is clear that the assumption that the cost of The Cherries would be lower than alternative, staffed accommodation, is justified.

It is also clear that costs of a full, ordinary house used as a group home would be lower still, since the elements in The Cherries costs of such things as rates and ground rent are based on a twelve-bedded unit. The matter of an economic rent, i.e. one which covers all costs, is confounded by the under-occupancy of The Cherries making such a charge a practical impossibility. Even with a full occupancy however, a further limiting factor is the fact that most of The Cherries residents came from the hostel. The rent charged in the group home therefore, had to be considerably less than that charged at the hostel since the latter provided many services including food that The Cherries residents would have to pay for separately. Since the rents charged at hostels are always much less than the full economic cost, it was almost certain that the rent charged at The Cherries would be less than economic.

This review of how The Cherries project achieved its objectives thus ends as it began, with favourable things being found for The Cherries as a group home and unfavourable things for The Cherries as a specific building. We would like to conclude with a suggestion, primarily aimed at our friends in Berkshire Social Services Department and, in particular the Slough Division, as to what might be done with The Cherries building in the future. It is now serving a function as a sort of 'half-way house' between staffed accommodation and council housing. We are not totally convinced of the necessity for a half-way stage but, in any case, would suggest a better utilization of The Cherries building could be achieved, for example, at the small additional cost of converting the building into three self-contained flats. Then at least the physical problems of a house for twelve people should be reduced, and a better utilization of what is, after all, a scarce resource, could be achieved.

CHAPTER X

Group homes and the mentally handicapped

"Tell me whom you live with, and I will tell you who you are" Spanish Proverb

Having considered the performance of The Cherries against its stated objectives, we end the book by looking at group homes in the wider context of residential provision for mentally handicapped adults. Behind the more specific objectives dealt with in the previous chapter were two aims. These were described in Chapter II as being to discover:

"1. Whether mentally handicapped people can live without supervision
 2. How low an I.Q. a person can have and still live in this way?"

In stating that The Cherries has fulfilled these aims, in that, clearly, mentally handicapped people have lived without supervision, and that someone with as low an I.Q. as 41–45 has lived in this way, one is at the same time learning the fundamental lesson of the project and, paradoxically, learning very little. We have, in the course of a number of discussions about group homes and The Cherries project, discovered an amazing range of awareness and opinion about the subject. There are some who, having no example of a group home in their area, and sometimes only just having had a hostel built, regard the project as a great breakthrough, and wish to replicate it in every detail. There are others who, having seen a number of group home developments over the years, regard The Cherries as an oversized anachronism. Between these two extremes fall most people, who vaguely support the idea of independent living and think that group homes are a 'good thing' but would restrict them to a very small, and very able, group of the mentally handicapped population.

For those who remain unconvinced that mentally handicapped people can live without residential supervision we therefore set The Cherries up as an example that they can and that in the main they mature and gain in confidence from the experience of independent living. For the group in the middle, we would stress most strongly the range of abilities which The Cherries, despite its physical limitations, managed to deal with, and would urge that group homes are not confined only to those with a superior practical competence. To the last group, we would send a reminder that everything has to start somewhere.

In the debate about residential accommodation for the mentally handicapped we would hope that first of all the argument is removed from what sort of *building* the accommodation is provided in, to what

95

sort of *care* is provided in that building. The Cherries, by being the 'wrong' building for the sort of care it was trying to provide, illustrates the folly of associating a particular type of care with a particular type of building. It seems to us totally unnecessary to have purpose-built accommodation for group homes, and we would strongly recommend the use of normal housing for this purpose. In saying that, however, we do not subscribe to the point of view, which many authorities seem to have accepted, that ordinary housing can only provide the sort of 'independent' care given to group homes. There are certainly a number of people now in hostel and hospital care who could be accommodated in, and benefit from, an independent group home in ordinary housing. There are still more, we feel, for whom varying levels of staffing are necessary, but who do not need purpose built accommodation in which to live.

Two examples can be given here, one from this country, and one from Sweden. In Sweden, the term 'group home' is used to describe a loose collection of between two and six self-contained flats within an ordinary residential block. One of these flats is normally kept as a 'base' flat, where the one staff member responsible for the group will have a small office and prepare meals for the least able of the group. The total size of the 'group' thus supervised will range between ten and thirty people, depending on the number of flats available, and the involvement of the staff member with the individuals will depend on the degree of independence they have achieved. Thus residents newly arrived from more sheltered residential care may need a considerable input of staff time to begin with, whereas others, who have been in their flat for some time, may only refer to the staff member occasionally. All such group homes are, as indicated above, in ordinary blocks of flats, and will not necessarily be grouped all together physically. The remainder of the flats in the block are occupied by perfectly ordinary families. Thus staffed accommodation in ordinary housing is achieved.

Group homes of the type described above are universal in Sweden. In England it is necessary to go to individual examples of ordinary housing being used with some resident staff input, since this is the exception rather than the rule. A few cases from our experience are: the use of one half of a semi-detached house by a group of residents, and the other half by a married couple, acting as staff; the sharing of a house between a group of students and a group of mentally handicapped adults; the various experiments under the auspices of the "L'Arche" charity. We are also delighted to see the beginnings of an experiment, in Wales, where ordinary housing, staffed appropriately, is being tried for *all* the mentally handicapped in the area.

These examples show that more independent living than that provided in purpose-built accommodation is possible, even if some resident staff are thought necessary. In emphasizing the value of group homes, then, we are talking about a particular type of care, not a particular type of building.

It will be clear, by now, that the major reason why we feel benefits have occurred to the residents of The Cherries is the sheer independence of group home living. This is emphasized throughout the book and is most clearly demonstrated by the effective use of the hostel, a less independent environment, as a deterrent against misbehaviour. Quite simply, the residents were happier deciding what they should do, rather than being told. This independence of action in the group home setting does however force into the open the problems of parents deciding how best to provide for their offspring, and adds a new dimension to the already difficult choices they have to make.

One point which may not have been noticed earlier is the lack, in The Cherries project, of direct movement from the parental home to The Cherries. Given that the project was originated by Slough Mencap, a parent's organization, it is surprising, looking back to Tables 3 and 4 in the previous chapter, that all those except Mary who got as far as being regular weekend visitors were considered as potential residents when either in hostel or hospital. Permanent care with parents had thus already ceased to exist. It is true that the original list put forward by Slough Mencap did contain some names of those living at home, but it is also true that there was no obvious pressure from any parents for their offspring to move to The Cherries. Anxieties over the experimental nature of the home could account for most of this reluctance, certainly in the early days of the experiment, but in addition perhaps there was a reluctance on the part of the Social Services to alter stable home situations when resources were scarce. Beyond these reasons, however, we feel that a more fundamental problem exists. This involves a whole spectrum of emotions, and is concerned both with parents 'letting their children go' in general, and with the greater problems this presents when the 'child' is mentally handicapped. Most of us have seen perfectly normal families, where one or both parents still seek to maintain parental control and exercise rights of decision over fully grown adults. On the other hand, we will also have seen parents who cast out their offspring to fend for themselves at a very early age. As usual the bulk of the population of parents are in the middle of the spectrum, trying to maintain family contacts whilst allowing a maturing adult to gradually assert his or her independence.

The problem of children growing up and leaving home is much more acute for parents of the mentally handicapped. As a number of studies have shown some parents will go to inordinate lengths to prevent their children being 'put away', although this was more prevalent a few years ago when the only choice for residential care was hospitalization. It is still extremely difficult, however, to try and persuade such parents of an adult's right to determine his or her own life, particularly if that adult continues to exhibit signs of dependency. Yet it could be argued that parents should be encouraged to let their offspring go into a group home when they are still capable of coping with them in their own home. The argument would take the form that it would be better in the long run, in that the mentally handicapped person will have achieved a greater maturity and independence by the time parents are too old to cope, and easier to achieve in the short-term, in that parental support through visiting and reassurance would smooth the transition from home to group home. The force of this argument will depend a lot on individual parent's attitude to their responsibilities and a hard objective look by them at the future for their children. We suspect however that, like many things, a few examples might add to the logic and the problem remains of who is willing to be the guinea pig.

Underneath all the arguments about group homes and residential accommodation, therefore, are fundamental problems about rights; rights of the mentally handicapped individual, and rights of his family. If the desirability of a normal life is accepted for the mentally handicapped then this carries with it certain rights of freedom of choice over actions, and associations with other people. It also includes the likelihood of being unhappy, and the possibility of being the object of control by other individuals. These more negative features of a normal life should not be forgotten by pretending that freedom from residential supervision is everything. On the whole, however, and to summarise the conclusions of this book we would advocate the greatest possible freedoms to be given to mentally handicapped adults and this must mean a considerable increase in the number of group homes.

Further experimentation is needed to determine the precise proportion of such homes in the total system of residential care, but it is clear that they now have far too small a part. If nothing else, the sheer economy of group homes may give them something of a priority in future allocations of resources. We would prefer, of course, that the tangible benefits to mentally handicapped adults, which we have observed at first hand in the experience of The Cherries will persuade many more authorities to develop the possibilities of group homes to the full.

We also hope that in such developments, this book will prove useful to those who, unlike The Cherries residents and staff, are not at a 'first beginning'.

Assessments of those resident in The Cherries for at least one year*

In order to give a more standardized view of The Cherries residents' abilities this appendix gives the results of various assessments of each of those eight residents of The Cherries who lived in the home for at least one year of the period of our study. These assessments were undertaken by the social workers attached to the group home, and by an independent psychologist. The psychologist used four tests to assess the abilities of the group: Peabody Picture Vocabulary, Kohs Blocks, Porteus Mazes, and Reynells Verbal Comprehension and Expressive Language Test. No results are given for the fourth test in this case since everyone's ability was above the upper limit (mental age = 7 years) but the I.Q. ranges obtained from the other tests are given together with brief comments on the results by the psychologist.

The assessments of the social workers used two completions of Gunzburg's Progress Assessment Charts of social and personal development (P.A.C.2)[60]. These charts list thirty activities in each of the fields of self-help, communication and socialization, and twelve in the occupational section. The skills are used as a check list, i.e. a person is credited with a skill only if they can carry out the whole of the activity mentioned. Thus the highest score anyone can have is 30 on the first three sections and 12 on the last. The scores have not been converted into the social competence index described by Gunzburg because of the difficulty of placing The Cherries residents in categories according to their I.Q.'s. As will be seen from the following pages these I.Q. scores vary considerably between the different tests used.

As well as the P.A.C. scores, Personal Assessments are given for each person, using further charts by Gunzburg. He says of the method:

"The slant of this particular assessment method is towards 'community tolerance'." The five points of each aspect must not be regarded as representing a continuum from a theoretically 'best' towards a theoretically 'worst' behaviour. In other words, the explanatory comments attached to the five-point scale of each subsection are indicative of behaviour which can either be just tolerated or will make a person fit reasonably well into his community or of such a nature that people cannot or will not put up with it.

A personal assessment is, therefore, particularly important when considering the personal relationships of a mentally handicapped person with people who will not make allowances for his handicap – i.e. the 'open' community. From this point of view a 'good' or high score should be given to behaviour which does not attract undue attention, which is unobtrusive, fits in well with

---

* This appendix is a shortened version of a paper which appeared in *The British Journal of Mental Subnormality*, Vol. XXIV, Part I, 1978.

the usual activities, is 'average' and does not require supervision nor causes concern even though there is still need for the helping hand and guidance. On the other hand, a 'poor' or low score must be given to behaviour which is offensive or criminal and which, whatever the reasons, results in rejection of the deviant by the community. This may lead to segregation by sending him to institutions or prison or prescribing special treatment and training, because such a person cannot be absorbed in the ordinary world whilst he displays such non-conforming behaviour. Also in this category of 'poor' scores are found people who need much attention and help, such as the extremely physically handicapped, because their dependence requires a more than ordinary degree of tolerance."

Each assessment is concluded with a summary based on comments made by the psychologist, social workers and others about the personality and abilities of the person concerned. The assessments are presented in alphabetical order of pseudonym.

BARBARA

Intelligence Test scores

Test	I.Q. Range
Peabody Picture Vocabulary	61–65
Kohs Blocks	51–55
Porteus Mazes	36–40
Average I.Q. range	51–55

The following remarks about these results were made by the psychologist who administered the tests:

"*Peabody* – Barbara's level of vocabulary was exceedingly good for her intellectual level, partly, I imagine, a result of the group home, and partly of working in the community.

"*Kohs* – She started well on the blocks and tried to be organized but became really confused when the designs were rotated through 45°. She was often not happy with her attempts, which she sometimes changed, but on other occasions implied it was the best she could do.

"*Mazes* – She seemed to quite enjoy the mazes although she needed reassuring over the 'waste of paper' when she had to begin again following an error! She sometimes repeated an error on her second attempt although she knew perfectly well it was wrong. Thus I feel her score on this test under-estimates her actual ability, which I would have thought was more on a level with the result of the Kohs blocks."

P.A.C.2 scores

	March 75	December 75
Self-Help	29	29
Communication	14	25
Socialization	28	28
Occupation	11	10

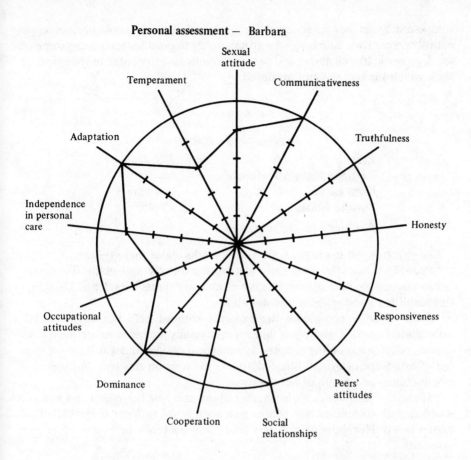

Personal assessment — Barbara

The main change seen over the nine months was Barbara's increased ability in the field of communication. This was influenced, not by the use of any specific training programme, but by each member of the group having to undertake more responsibility for their day to day lives as the social workers tried to limit the time and number of their visits. In addition the employment situation had an effect since those residents, like Barbara, who still had outside employment, were aware of the need for increased effort if they, too, were not to be made redundant. (It should be noted here, however, that some of the improvement was caused, as it was with every other member in the group, by the two pairs of social workers differing slightly in interpretation and occasionally the later pair recording the capabilities of the group rather than whether these abilities were used. For example the reading level of most of the group was fairly high even though Doreen was the only one who read books regularly.)

Barbara's personal assessment, with several '5' ratings, indicated that she did not have many problems fitting into society. Her temperament, which leads to occasional outbursts of aggression, did not cause severe problems and her occupational attitude was sufficient to enable her to hold down her job with little difficulty. It is interesting, however, that only one major problem, her drinking, prevented her from moving on to the council house.

Barbara is a very friendly but sometimes very obstinate person, who tends to be lazy in The Cherries when the others let her. She is relatively steady and

101

competent given her intellectual limitations, but could probably not cope entirely on her own. She needed a group, partly to prod her into doing some of the dirty work, like cleaning, and partly to compensate for some of the practical skills which she had still not mastered.

CATHY

Intelligence Test scores

Test	I.Q. Range
Peabody Picture Vocabulary	66–70
Kohs Blocks	less than 35
Porteus Mazes	41–45
Average I.Q. range	46–50

The psychologist made the following remarks about these results:

"*Peabody* – Cathy considered each word carefully and made few errors before she reached her ceiling. She is well able to express herself and I feel that this result is a good reflection of her ability.

"*Kohs* – Cathy completed the example without help but began to fail immediately on the test designs. She seemed totally unable to relate the blocks to each other, even on the simplest symmetrical design, and was unaware that her efforts were incorrect. She did appear nervous on this test, but was also rather clumsy as a result of her spasticity.

"*Mazes* – Cathy was a little happier about this test but continued to look worried. She completed the Mazes successfully up to Year 6 but failed all higher levels. Her drawing was very shaky – again I assume as a result of her spasticity."

P.A.C.2 scores

	March 75	December 75
Self-Help	28	29
Communication	19	30
Socialization	27	28
Occupation	7	6

Like every other member of the group except Martin, Cathy improved her 'social competence' over the measured period, especially in communication. This broad heading covers such things as coping with money and ability to measure time, distance, etc., as well as the normal communication skills of reading, writing, etc., and it was in these aspects that Cathy made the most marked progress. Her fairly low score in the occupation section can be attributed to her physical disability which leads to unsteadiness and lack of dexterity.

Cathy's personal assessment shows that she does not have much difficulty in fitting into the society in which she lives and works. Her generally quiet and retiring nature is indicated by lower scores in occupational attitudes and dominance which do cause some slight worry when looked at in relation to Richard's personality, because he can be very dominating. However as yet this has caused no major problems and the minor ones have becomes less frequent

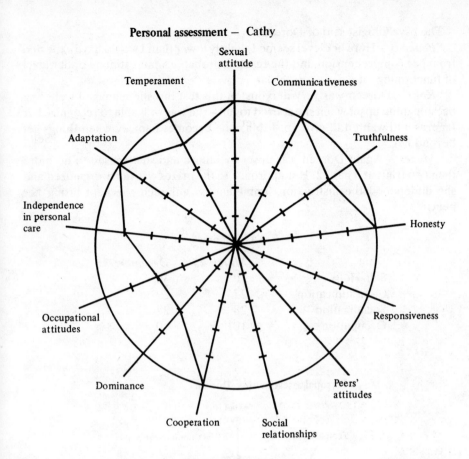

Personal assessment — Cathy

- Sexual attitude
- Communicativeness
- Truthfulness
- Honesty
- Responsiveness
- Peers' attitudes
- Social relationships
- Cooperation
- Dominance
- Occupational attitudes
- Independence in personal care
- Adaptation
- Temperament

as the marriage has developed and the couple have settled into their new situation.

Cathy is likeable and willing but worries a great deal about every little problem that arises even though, practically, she is fairly competent. She also has a fairly narrow unimaginative outlook on life. For example she feels that as a married woman she should look after Richard and do all the housework, and thus she was upset when the group suggested that Richard should do his share of cleaning of the communal rooms, because she felt that this would involve her in doing twice as much work as the others. Another example of her lack of imagination is her provision of bread and butter sandwiches every day for Richard's lunch.

DOREEN

Intelligence Test scores

Test	I.Q. Range
Peabody Picture Vocabulary	61–65
Kohs Blocks	61–65
Porteus Mazes	56–60
Average I.Q. Range	56–60

The psychologist said of Doreen:

"*Peabody* – Here her level seemed slightly lower than I would have expected from her comprehension, but the result is probably a fair estimate of her level of functioning.

"*Kohs* – Doreen was very nervous on this test but she managed well. She became quite upset when she started to fail – she was well able to recognize her failures and wanted to give up. I think she becomes panicky when things get beyond her.

"*Mazes* – Again Doreen was upset by failure and she refused to do more than two trials at Year 12. Her approach to the mazes was fairly organized and she understood the instructions immediately, although she kept lifting her pencil."

P.A.C.2 scores

	March 75	December 75
Self-Help	30	30
Communication	23	29
Socialization	28	27
Occupation	10	10

Personal assessment – Doreen

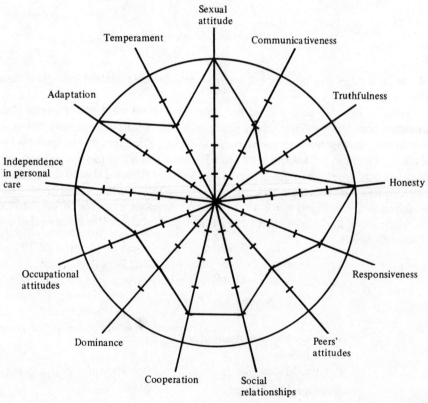

Once again the improvement seen over the nine month period was in the field of communication. The change was partly caused by the way Doreen had 'blossomed' in the group home taking up several hobbies, such as reading, which had been abandoned during the period of training and introduction to the group home. She had also learnt to manage her money with greater ease, though she did find it difficult to manage on supplementary benefit after having been in receipt of a much higher weekly wage. The general impression given by these scores is of a very capable person and this did give rise to the suggestion that Doreen might be capable of managing completely on her own. However, her personal assessment suggests that there would be certain problems here.

Her main problem is that she is not particularly popular amongst her 'superiors', i.e. staff. Despite getting on fairly well with her peers, she also likes attention from the former group and her only way of getting attention seems to be by telling 'stories' or creating an argument or fight. Although this does not happen as frequently as it used to, it still seems to make Doreen too unstable to be able to cope by herself. Another aspect of her character which would be far more of a problem in an individual setting than in the group home is her lack of persistence. She will give up very easily at the first sign of trouble or difficulty and can sometimes only be persuaded to do things after much hard work. This persuasion has to be fairly gentle as she can also be obstinate though this does not present the group with as many problems as Barbara's stubbornness.

MARTIN

Intelligence Test scores

Test	I.Q. Range
Peabody Picture Vocabulary	56–60
Kohs Blocks	less than 35
Porteus Mazes	46–50
Average I.Q. Range	41–45

The psychologist made the following remarks about these results:

"*Peabody* – Martin's vocabulary was surprisingly large, although he tended to make mistakes on easy words and then succeed on harder ones.

"*Kohs* – Martin managed to complete the example but thereafter was absolutely lost. He was easily satisfied with wrong solutions and didn't even spend time finding the correct colours, e.g. he would happily use a blue and yellow side when a plain blue was required. His score was therefore 0 and this gives a mental age of less than 5 years 3 months (I.Q. less than 35).

"*Mazes* – Here, Martin had rather more idea of what was required but he could not cope with the more complicated mazes. However he would have continued quite happily – he was unconcerned by failure.

"*Reynell* – I thought perhaps he might need to be assessed on this but he completed the final sections of the test adequately and so his abilities obviously are above the test ceiling.

Personal assessment — Martin

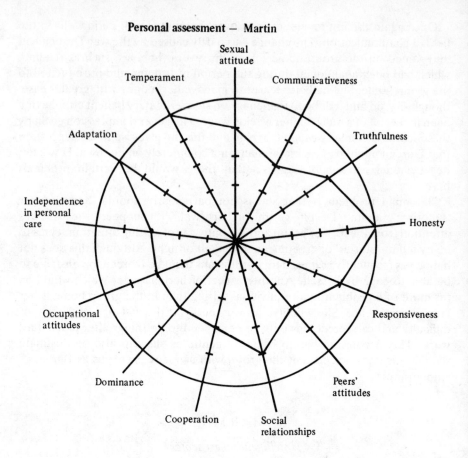

P.A.C.2 scores

	March 75	December 75
Self-Help	18	18
Communication	6	3
Socialization	23	15
Occupation	7	5

Martin was the only member of the group whose abilities showed a general decline over the nine month period. As the group became more stable they, and in this case Mary in particular, were able to give Martin more support of which he took full advantage, and thus his abilities *as an individual* have declined. He and Mary have built quite a strong relationship based on Mary helping Martin with most of his cooking and shopping, but using him to do odd jobs for her in return.

Martin's assessment does, in fact, highlight one of the major problems of using the P.A.C in this group situation because it does not make any allowance for shared skills. For example Cathy and Richard are far more capable as a pair than either of them is individually, but since both now rely on the other to do some of the things that they found especially difficult, they are not in theory maximizing their individual potential. However we feel that, since very few 'normal' human beings ever maximize their potential ability to perform all everyday tasks, The Cherries residents and other group home members must be allowed to be 'normal' and depend on others if there is mutual agreement about the acceptability of such dependency.

To return to Martin his personal assessment shows that not only are his practical capabilities somewhat limited, but that his personality would make it difficult for him to manage alone, even though he has no very low ratings. This is not therefore because of any major disabilities, but more because he is fairly quiet and retiring most of the time and will not often speak up for himself, despite his fairly extensive vocabulary. He does sometimes get into a very 'silly' mood and 'act the goat' as the other residents say. This they find very upsetting when it happens in public because it gets them noticed and one thing that the whole group wants is to be able to live in a community without being labelled as different.

However, because Martin is very pleasant and helpful the group are prepared to help and tolerate him. He is also very good natured which means that he is often asked to run odd errands which other residents do not feel like doing.

MARY

Intelligence Test scores

Test	I.Q. Range
Peabody Picture Vocabulary	86–90
Kohs Blocks	56–60
Porteus Mazes	101–105
Average I.Q. Range	80–85

The psychologist made the following remarks about Mary's attitude to these tests:

"*Peabody* – Mary began in a bad temper but settled as this became harder and therefore a challenge. She was not upset by her eventual failure as she regarded the words had by then become 'useless' to her (e.g. hieroglyphic, genealogist). She obviously did not feel deprived for not knowing them!

"*Kohs* – I was most surprised by her failure on this test. She couldn't really bring herself to concentrate (i.e. her interest wasn't sufficiently stimulated) but she had little success even when she tried. Once the designs were rotated 45° she insisted she needed five blocks and after spending about one minute on each design, she refused to continue. Mary's spatial organization is obviously poor in relation to her other abilities.

"*Mazes* – In contrast to her approach to the Kohs, Mary really entered into the spirit of the Mazes. She completed them fairly quickly but was also exceedingly accurate – she managed the Adult mazes on the first attempt.

P.A.C.2 scores

	March 75	December 75
Self-Help	28	30
Communication	28	30
Socialization	29	27
Occupation	12	12

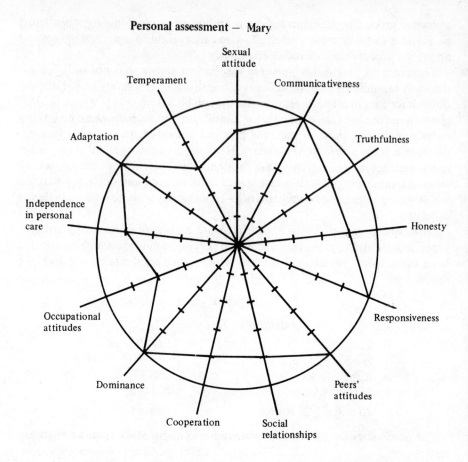

Personal assessment — Mary

As can be seen from the above scores and from the intelligence test results, Mary was the most competent resident of The Cherries. Her practical skills are definitely great enough to enable her to cope on her own, but she does not have the personality to enable her to do this. The only sections in the P.A.C. where she was not positively credited are those about being friendly and polite, because Mary is very verbally aggressive and suspicious.

The personal assessment also shows that Mary's main problem is her temperament, which seems to have arisen as a result of family problems. She is very insecure and a great worrier, which means that she needs both the social workers and the group to give her confidence. When the two new social workers took over responsibility for the group home they felt at first that Mary constituted a destructive emotional force. They soon came to realize that, while the group might be more successful without Mary, she could certainly not manage without the group. She needs to feel capable and in charge and in a less handicapped group her emotional problems would be far greater because she would be less sure of her ability to cope.

Also, despite giving the group more problems that they might otherwise have, Mary is probably necessary for Martin to survive in the group, since she is the one who gives him the most help. Admittedly, if she was ill or away for a while the others, particularly Doreen, would help Martin, but it is doubtful whether they would be able or prepared to do this all the time. Thus it is again obvious that the group situation enabled The Cherries residents to function successfully in the community where, as individuals, they might not survive.

Since living in The Cherries Mary has become more aware of her problems and is beginning to learn to control her temper and aggression. She has now progressed to the stage where, if she feels upset or angry, she will take herself away from the situation to somewhere where she can be quiet in order to calm down. This is a distinct improvement from the aggression that she used to use. However, Mary still has many personality problems to overcome, if she is ever to have the self-confidence to live entirely on her own. Indeed, it may be questionable whether such a final solution is entirely desirable in any case, in view of her interactions with the others in the group.

RICHARD

Intelligence Test scores

Test	I.Q. Range
Peabody Picture Vocabulary	81–85
Kohs Blocks	51–55
Porteus Mazes	71–75
Average I.Q. range	66–70

The psychologist said of Richard:

"*Peabody* – This test took an unbelievably long time. The harder the vocabulary became, the more Richard rose to the challenge, working on each alternative and refusing to move on until each picture had been resolved to his satisfaction. His score is a fair estimate of his awareness of words for he knows of many words without having a full grasp of their meaning. However, his daily usage of language, although impressive, is not as good as the Peabody score would suggest.

"*Kohs* – Richard worked at an average rate on this test. He again rose to the challenge of more difficult designs (completing them faster and more efficiently) but he could not cope with the 45° rotation and failed thereafter.

"*Mazes* – Again Richard rose to the challenge, succeeding at higher levels through thought and perseverance, where a degree of carelessness had resulted in failure at lower levels. His results on this test appeared to be a good reflection of his general level of ability."

P.A.C.2 scores

	March 75	December 75
Self-Help	30	30
Communication	20	29
Socialization	25	22
Occupation	10	6

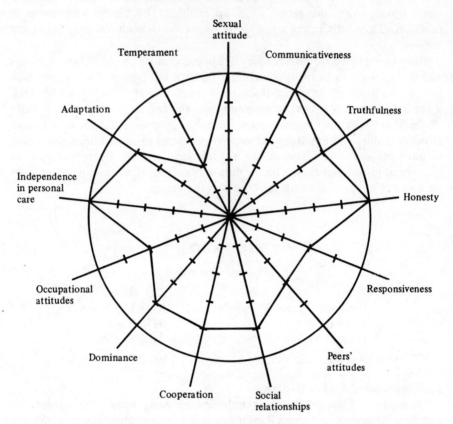

As with nearly all the other Cherries residents, Richard achieved a general improvement in coping with money and using different forms of communication over the nine months. However, he did not show such a high level of social competence in the other sections of the P.A.C. and this was, according to the social workers, purely as a result of his marriage.

Cathy and Richard both have a fairly old fashioned view of marriage in that the man should provide the money and the woman should do all the work about the house. This they held to despite the fact that Cathy was the one who brought home most of the money, and it is this attitude which led to so much of their money worries when they were first married. It also meant that Richard no longer did as much cooking or washing, despite them being well within his capabilities. However, he did do most of the shopping because he realized that Cathy's spasticity made it difficult for her to carry heavy shopping bags.

Richard is intellectually far more capable than Cathy but his personal assessment shows that he has problems that would mean he would have far more difficulty in fitting into the open community. He has always had a tendency to be aggressive and this is always increased when he feels threatened by problems that arise, and when he is not allowed to do things in his own way at his own speed.

ROGER

Intelligence Test scores

Test	I.Q. Range
Peabody Picture Vocabulary	61–65
Kohs Blocks	61–65
Porteus Mazes	66–70
Average I.Q. Range	66–70

The following remarks were made, by the psychologist, about Roger and his test results:

"*Peabody* – Roger was fairly competent on this test and resisted guessing, telling me the words were hard and he had never heard of them. His manner on all the tests was confident, and he appeared to regard himself as a competent individual.

"*Kohs* – Roger showed some nervousness here and it appeared to interfere with his concentration, but when he concentrated fully his results were surprisingly good and quickly completed.

"*Mazes* – Again Roger was rather blasé and as a result made a couple of silly errors thus depressing his score a little. His successes were in fact quite patchy (e.g. he succeeded at first attempt on Year 12, but failed Year 7 and needed two tries at Year 6)."

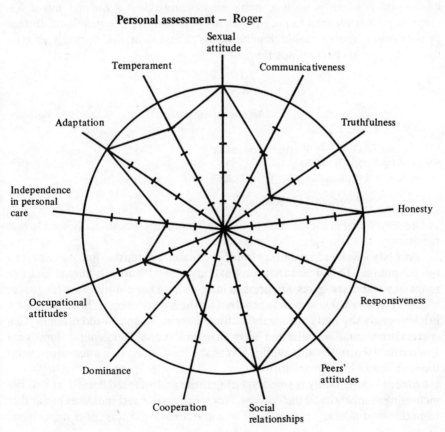

Personal assessment – Roger

	December 75
Self-Help	24
Communication	23
Socialization	19
Occupation	10

Roger, like Sally, had only been living in The Cherries for three months when these forms were completed, and thus neither of them had had time to react fully to the experience of living in the group home. Although their results are more comparable with the March 75 results for the rest of The Cherries group than with those for December 75, it is still difficult to make comparisons since by that time three of the early residents had been there for over a year, and only Doreen had lived there for less than six months. From his personal assessment it is seen that Roger has three major 'problems': he tends to be untruthful, he likes to throw his weight about, and he does not like washing. The group could cope with the first two problems without too much difficulty since Mary, at least, could dominate the whole group when the need arose. However nobody seemed to be able to instill into Roger a desire for cleanliness. This is a situation which might have led to Roger returning to the hostel, before more dramatic events took him elsewhere.

Roger was very lucky in having a job where personal appearance does not matter, because he is quite capable of holding down a normal job if his employers are prepared to put up with his personal hygiene problems. In fact he is definitely more capable than he seems at first sight, and this only adds to the tragedy of his current position.

SALLY

Intelligence Test scores

Test	I.Q. Range
Peabody Picture Vocabulary	51–55
Kohs Blocks	46–50
Porteus Mazes	86–90
Average I.Q. Range	61–65

The psychologist made the following comments about Sally's I.Q. test results:

"*Peabody* – Sally's vocabulary is not particularly extensive but she uses it to full advantage. Thus I feel that the Peabody result, though it may reflect her range of vocabulary, gives a depressed indication of her ability to use language.

"*Kohs* – Sally knew what was required on the Kohs but once she had placed a brick wrongly she had extreme difficulty in altering it, and would often move a correct brick out of position and leave an incorrect one. Her general clumsiness was particularly noticeable on this test as she made clutching attempts to keep the four bricks in a square format.

"*Mazes* – Sally really seemed to enjoy these and adapted herself well to the increasing complexity of the designs. Her score on this test indicates her ability to perform at a near average level in some areas, and was most impressive.

"*Reynell* – I did check her language levels on this test because of her poor result on the Peabody, but she answered every question well above the level required."

P.A.C.2 scores

	December 75
Self-Help	25
Communication	8
Socialization	17
Occupation	9

Sally was obviously not as competent as the rest of The Cherries group, apart from Martin, but she had made progress during the period up to December 1975, especially in using her initiative, both in practical situations and in conversation. The major skills which she had not yet mastered were those of coping with money, and therefore shopping, and reading.

The personal assessment shows that Sally does not have any serious problems in fitting into the community. She only scores on the 3 level on three ratings and these are all caused by her basic shyness and lack of communicative skills. The group home should help her quite considerably with both of these aspects.

Personal assessment – Sally

Sally is very friendly and cheerful and very willing, but is sometimes 'picked on' by the group because of her clumsiness. This is possibly caused by the fairly heavy doses of anti-convulsants which she takes to control her epilepsy, or by the epilepsy itself. She is also very quiet, and shy with strangers.

Group Assessment

The difficulties that arise in describing the capabilities of The Cherries residents are highlighted by the range in their I.Q. scores as measured by the three different tests. Obviously some variation is expected since the tests are measuring different aspects of 'intelligence', but the wide range seen, for example, in Sally's results, shows how wary one must be of classifying people on one test result. One interesting point which does arise, is the higher attainment shown by nearly everyone on the Peabody Picture Vocabulary test as compared with the rest. This is, perhaps, an indication of one of the effects of group home living.

From all the assessments it is possible to say that Mary is the most competent member of the group home, and that Martin is the least capable, but it would be impossible to rank the whole group in any meaningful way. Each member has their own special talents, and their own particular disabilities, and it was this combination of abilities which enabled the group to function as successfully as it did.

Costs of caring environments – details of calculation

This appendix shows how the cost figures, given in Chapter IX, of different caring environments are calculated. In any comparison of costs of care provision, an averaging process has to take place. This can sometimes preclude individual cases which defy the arguments produced by the averaging process, but, for the purposes of evaluating one of the fundamental elements of care provision, the overall effects of expenditure must dominate.

The analysis below considers the total cost of each caring environment to the state, as far as this can be ascertained. In comparing costs, it should, therefore, be borne in mind that costs accruing to families or employers have not been considered, but still have to be met. In planning services, however, the cost to the state will usually prove decisive and it is for this reason that this is the cost primarily used. It is possible, of course, to divide the 'state' into various parts, e.g. Local and National Government, Social Security and National Health Service, and it may be useful elsewhere to consider the costs of care to each part. However, in this appendix costs are considered as paid by the tax/rate payer as a single entity. The main environments discussed in the book, i.e. hostel, hospital, home, group home, A.T.C. and open employment as they form into living and working segments are the ones being compared. Information on cost figures was obtained from various authorities in Berkshire.

The comparison is restricted to revenue costs, i.e. the recurring costs over time of running the various environments. Justification for this particular form of costing is given in Chapter IX. Varying amounts of detail are available on the recurrent costs of services provided. These are usually presented under two major headings, direct and indirect costs. Direct costs are defined as those costs that can be directly and easily attributed to a specific environment, e.g. the salary of staff members, the gas bill, etc. Indirect costs are much more difficult to define, still more so to allocate. Thus the cost of administering residential services in Social Services Departments should be recognized in the costs of a hostel, since that administration has some effect on the hostel, but a specific proportion is difficult to decide upon. Even more remote from the actual environment, how much of the salary of a local Director of Social Services can be allocated to any one of his establishments? This tends to become a matter of local costing practice and, in some places, indirect costs tend to be allocated to a particular establishment in the same ratio that its direct costs are to the direct costs of all establishments of that type. In others allocation is carried out simply on the ratio of its beds to the total beds. Thus if one hostel has a quarter of the *direct costs* of all hostels, it may be allocated one quarter of the administrative costs of hostels. On the other hand if it had one third of the *hostel beds available*, it might be allocated one quarter of the administrative costs. Since this local practice does vary, indirect costs will not be included in the comparison, although some reference may be made to them in passing.

With this in mind the analysis of costs will now be presented, taking each environment in turn.

Costs of 'Home' Environments

For those living at home two environments are considered. These are home/A.T.C. and home/open employment. Our definitions of costs to 'the state' mean that the home/open employment person effectively has zero cost. For those at A.T.C.s two charges arise. First, the cost of the A.T.C. itself and, second, a charge to the Social Security Department in the form of Supplementary Benefit.

A.T.C. Costs

The accounts for 1974/75 for Berkshire Social Services Department show a revenue cost of £299,463 for the A.T.C.s under its control. This cost is net of revenue produced by the A.T.C.s. If the capital element (known as debt charges) of £47,058 is removed this leaves a total *direct* revenue cost of £252,405. Average attendance at A.T.C.s during this year was 492, giving an annual direct revenue cost of £513.02 per person per year, of £9.87 per week.

Supplementary Benefit Costs

For those living at home, payment of Supplementary Benefit is dependent on whether the person is over 18 and has been drawing benefit for a continuous period of two years or more. In October 1974 this benefit was £8.40 per week if under 80, plus an allowance of 90p for rent. Those aged 16 or 17 claim on the 'Ordinary' scale, as do those over 18 who have not been claiming for two years or more. The latter category are assumed to be minimal, since trainees tend to come straight from school at sixteen. Thus the rate for 16 and 17 year olds is the only other one to be considered, and this was £5.15 plus 90p for rent.

The average cost of supplementary benefits to the home/A.T.C. group thus depends on the proportion of those under 18 attending A.T.C.s. A figure of 6%, obtained from an original 'census' of services in Berkshire, will be used here. Thus for the A.T.C. group the average cost per week of supplementary benefit was $(8.40 + 0.90) \times 0.94 + (5.15 + 0.90) \times 0.06 = £9.10$.

Total costs of 'Home' environments 1974/75

Environment	Elements of cost per week		Total cost per week £
Home/open employment	none		nil
Home/A.T.C.	A.T.C. cost	9.87	
	Supplementary benefit cost	9.10	
		18.97	18.97

Cost of 'Hospital' environments 1974/75

The only available cost information on hospital environments is an all embracing average, regardless of whether the individuals are working or note, and thus a cost is given to cover all environments. For the two hospitals in Berkshire the costs were £54.60 and £49.70 per patient week. Using a weighted average to allow for the relative numbers in each hospital, this gives an average cost per week as follows:

Environment	Total cost per week
Hospital	£51.34

Costs of 'Hostel' environments

Here two possible environments are considered. These are hostel/A.T.C. and hostel/open employment. In the first of these, three costs have to be considered. The cost of the hostel, the cost of the A.T.C., and the supplementary benefit cost. For hostel/open employment people only the hostel costs need to be considered.

Hostel costs 1974/75

The accounts for 1974/75 show a net cost of £171,293 for the county's hostels, including the contributions of residents. Removing the debt charges of £62,584 the total direct revenue cost of hostel provision in 1974/75 was £108,709. The average occupancy during this period is given as 103 and thus the average cost per resident of hostel care was £1055.43 per year, or £20.30 per week.

A.T.C. costs

These are the same as those calculated for the home/A.T.C. group, i.e. £9.87 per week.

Supplementary Benefit costs

The Supplementary Benefits Commission treats people in Local Authority residential accommodation as a special category, paying them at the same rate as the flat rate old age pension. In 1974/75 this was £10 per week for all hostel residents not in open employment.

Total costs of 'Hostel' environments 1974/75

Environment	Elements of cost per week		Total cost per week £
Hostel/open employment	hostel costs	20.30	
		20.30	20.30
Hostel/A.T.C.	hostel costs	20.30	
	A.T.C. cost	9.87	
	Supplementary benefit cost	10.00	
		40.17	40.17

117

Costs of 'Group Home' environments

Residents of The Cherries had, like hostel residents, two alternative living/working environments. These are group home/open employment and group home/A.T.C. Also like hostel residents, the former group have only the group home costs to consider, whereas the latter have to add the cost of the A.T.C. and the Supplementary Benefit costs.

Group home costs

In attempting to arrive at a fair figure for comparison, our early reports on The Cherries used estimates from Slough Social Services for the costs of The Cherries with an occupancy for 10 people. This was because a full year's costs with such an occupancy level were not available. This as we have seen is unfortunately still the case, since the home is yet to be completely filled, and thus the group home 'costs' which follow are still estimates. The only estimates available are those for 1975/76, since 1974/75 estimates were not amalgamated into the Berkshire system following reorganization. If anything, therefore, the costs used will be an overestimate, although they are, to some extent, based on expenditure during 1974/75. The distinction is made between the cost of the home with and without the cost of social worker and home help assistance, although it appears increasingly likely that some element of social worker time would have to be included in a realistic assessment of the home's cost. We have also reduced the expected occupancy level to six, in line with the likely outcomes described in Chapter IX.

The 1975/76 revenue estimates give a figure of £3290 for the direct cost of the home, i.e. ground rent, rates, maintenance, depreciation of furniture and fittings, and fuel. The cost of the social worker and home help (using wage levels appropriate to 1974/75) is estimated at £3490. With an occupancy of 6, this gives a figure of £10.54 per resident per week, or £21.72 if social worker and home help time is included.

The rent at the time was £5.25, and thus the net cost of group home residence is estimated at either $(£10.54 - £5.25) = £5.29$ or $(£21.72 - £5.25) = £16.47$ depending on the inclusion or exclusion of social worker and home help time.

A.T.C. costs

These are the same as for the home/A.T.C. and hostel/A.T.C. group, i.e. £9.87 per week's attendance.

Supplementary Benefit costs

The 'normal' situation of group home residents attending the A.T.C.s is that they are placed in the same category as ordinary single people living in rented accommodation. This entitled them, on the 'long term' scale, to a benefit of £10.40 in 1974/75 plus an allowance for rent. The rent allowance covers the full rent paid less a notational amount of £1.80 for the fuel, etc. elements thereof. Thus the total supplementary benefit cost of a group home resident attending the A.T.C. was, in 1974/75, $£10.40 + £5.25 - £1.80 = £13.85$ per week.

Total costs of 'Group House' environments (assuming average occupancy of 6 residents)

Environment	Elements of cost per week		Total cost per week £
Group home/open employment (if SW and HH costs included)	Group home cost	15.47 15.47	15.47
Group home/open employment (if SW and HH costs excluded)	Group home cost	5.29 5.29	5.29
Group home/A.T.C. (if SW and HH costs included)	Group home cost A.T.C. cost Supplementary benefit cost	16.47 9.87 13.85 39.19	39.19
Group home/A.T.C. (if SW and HH costs excluded)	Group home cost A.T.C. cost Supplementary benefit cost	5.29 9.87 13.85 29.01	29.01

Taking these individual costs together, we arrive at Table 5 of Chapter IX, which compares the average cost per week to the 'state' of a mentally handicapped adult in each of the living/working environments listed.

References

1. Tredgold, A. F. (1909), The Feebleminded – A Social Danger, *Eugenics Review* 1, 97–104.

2. Tredgold, A. F. (1952), *A Text Book on Mental Deficiency (Amentia)*, 8th edition, London: Bailliere, Tindall & Cox.

3. O'Connor, N. (1965), The Successful Employment of the Mentally Handicapped. In Hilliard, L. T. and Kirman, B. H., *Mental Deficiency*, London: Churchill.

4. Mental Deficiency Committee (1929), *Wood Report*, London: HMSO.

5. Tredgold, A. F. (1952), op. cit.

6. Lyle, J. G. (1960), The Effect of an Institution Environment upon the Verbal Development of Imbecile Children. III. The Brooklands Residential Family Unit, *J. Ment. Def. Res.*, 4, 14–23.

7. Tizard, J. (1964), *Community Services for the Mentally Handicapped*, London: Oxford University Press.

8. National Council for Civil Liberties (1951), *50,000 Outside The Law*, London.

9. King Edward's Hospital Fund for London (1955), *Report on Mental Illness and Mental Deficiency Hospitals*, London.

10. Mental Health Act (1959), London: HMSO.

11. Baranjay, E. P. (1971), *The Mentally Handicapped Adolescent*, Oxford: Pergamon.

12. Department of Health and Social Security (1971), Command 4683: *Better Services for the Mentally Handicapped*, London: HMSO.

13. Department of Health and Social Security (1971), op. cit.

14. Morris, P. (1969), *Put Away: A Sociological Study of Institutions for the Mentally Retarded*, London: Routledge and Kegan Paul.

15. *Report of the Committee of Inquiry into Allegations of Ill-treatment of Patients and other Irregularities at the Ely Hospital, Cardiff* (1969), Howe Report, Command 3795, London: HMSO.

16. Home Office, Dept. of Education and Science, Ministry of Housing and Local Government, Ministry of Health (1968), *Report of the Committee on Local Authority and Allied Personal Social Services*, (The Seebohm Report), Command 3703, London: HMSO.

17. Campaign for the Mentally Handicapped (1971), *The White Paper and Future Services for the Mentally Handicapped*, London: CMH.

18. Campaign for the Mentally Handicapped (1972), *Even Better Services for the Mentally Handicapped*, London: CMH.

19. Elliott, J. (1972), Eight Propositions for Mental Handicap, *Brit. J. Ment. Subn.*, 18, Pt. 1.

20. R.M.P.A. (1971), R.M.P.A. Memorandum on Future Patterns of Care for the Mentally Subnormal, *Brit. J. Psychiat.*, 119.

21. Department of Health and Social Security (1976), *Priorities in the Health and Social Services in England – A Consultative Document*, London: HMSO.

22. Elliott, J. (1975), Segregated Ghetto or Better Services? *Res. Soc. Work.*, 15, 1.

23. Day, K. (1974), Follow the Northern Lights, *New Psychiatry*, 28 Nov.

24. Pilkington, T. L. (1964), Mental Subnormality in Great Britain, *Brit. J. Ment. Subn.*, 10, Pt. 2.

25. Gunzburg, H. C. (1973), The Role of the Psychologist in Manipulating the Institutional Environment. In Clarke, A. D. B. and Clarke, A. M. (eds), *Mental Retardation and Behavioural Research*, IRMR Study Group No. 4, London: Churchill Livingstone.

26. Kushlick, A., Felce, D., Palmer, J. and Smith, J. (1976), *Evidence to the Committee of Inquiry into Mental Handicap Nursing and Care from the Health Care Evaluation Research Team.*

27. Shapiro, A. (1974), Fact and Fiction in the Care of the Mentally Handicapped, *Brit. J. Psychiat.*, 125.

28. Shearer, A. (1972), Normalization? *C.M.H. Discussion Paper 3*, London: CMH.

29. Tyne, A. (1976), Handicap: A Rejoinder, *New Society*, 8 July 1976.

30. Williams, C. and Elliott, J. (1976), *Services for Mentally Handicapped Children*, King's Fund Centre, *Mental Handicap Papers*: 10, London.

31. Meacher, M. (1976), Living in Harmony, *Community Care*, 7 Jan. 1976.

32. Department of Health and Social Security (1976), op. cit.

33. Mittler, P. (1976), Priority for Handicap, *New Society*, 1 July 1976.

34. Francklin, S. (1973), Mentally Handicapped People Living in Ordinary Houses and Flats, *Centre on Environment for the Handicapped Papers No. 2*, London: CEH.

35. Clarke, A. D. B. (1976), From Research to Practice. *Presidential Address given to 4th Congress of Assn. Scient. Stud. Ment. Def.*, Washington, 1976.

36. *Report of the Care of Patients at South Ockenden Hospital* (1974), London: HMSO.

37. S. E. Thames R.H.A. (1976), *Report of Independent Committee of Inquiry into Allegations about the Care and Treatment of Mental Patients in the Long-Stay Wards at St. Augustines Hospital, Chartham Down.*

38. Department of Health and Social Security (1976), *The Facilities and Services of Mental Illness and Mental Handicap Hospitals in England and Wales*, Statistical and Research Report Series, No. 11, London: HMSO.

39. Nursing Times (1974), What is your Score? – 1, *Nursing Times*, 17 October 1974.

40. Jones, K., Brown, J., Cunningham, W. J., Roberts, J. and Williams, P. (1975), *Opening the Door. A Study of New Policy for the Mentally Handicapped*, London: Routledge and Kegan Paul.

41. Jones, K. et al. (1975), op. cit.

42. Royal College of Psychiatry (1976), Mental Deficiency Section: Memorandum on the Present and Future Development and Organization of Mental Handicap Services, *Brit. J. Psychiat.*, News and Notes, August 1976.

43. Jones, K. et al. (1975), op. cit.

44. Smith, G. (1975), Institutional Dependence is Reversible, *Social Work Today*, 16, 14.

45. Grunewald, K. (1974), *The Mentally Retarded in Sweden*, The Swedish Institute.

46. Robinson, J. and Sweeney, M. (1974), *The Cherries: A Group Home for the Mentally Handicapped. Progress Report to 31 March 1974*, Buckinghamshire County Council Social Services Department.

47. Robinson, J. and Sweeney, M. (1974), op. cit.

48. Robinson, J. and Sweeney, M. (1974), op. cit.

49. Robinson, J. and Sweeney, M. (1974), op. cit.

50. Gunzburg, H. C. (1960), *Social Rehabilitation of the Subnormal*, London: Bailliere, Tindall and Cox.

51. Tizard, J. (1964), op. cit.

52. Dickson, A. (1975), Restoring the right to a sex life, *New Psychiatry*, 5 June 1975.

53. Lee, G. W. and Katz, G. (1974), *Sexual Rights of the Retarded*, London: NSMHC.

54. Grunewald, K. (1974), op. cit.

55. Grunewald, K. (1974), op. cit.

56. Brunel Institute of Organization and Social Studies (1974), *Social Services Departments, Developing Patterns of Work and Organization*, London: Heinemann.

57. Race, D. G. and Race, D. M. (1976), The Price of Living in Harmony, *Community Care*, 1 September 1976.

58. Race, D. G. and Race, D. M. (1975), Investigation into the Effects of Different Caring Environments on the Social Competence of Mentally Handicapped Adults: *Progress Report No. 1 Reading: Operational Research (Health and Social Services) Unit.*

59. Race, D. G. & Race, D. M. (1976), Investigation into the Effects of Different Caring Environments on the Social Competence of Mentally Handicapped Adults: *Progress Report No. 2 Reading: Operational Research (Health and Social Services) Unit.*

60. Gunzburg, H. C. (1974), *The P-A-C Manual*, 3rd edition, London: NSMHC.

Printed in Great Britain for Her Majesty's Stationery Office
by J. W. Arrowsmith Ltd., Bristol BS2 3NT
Dd 597092 K16 5/79